The Sunday Brunch Cookbook

EBURY
PRESS

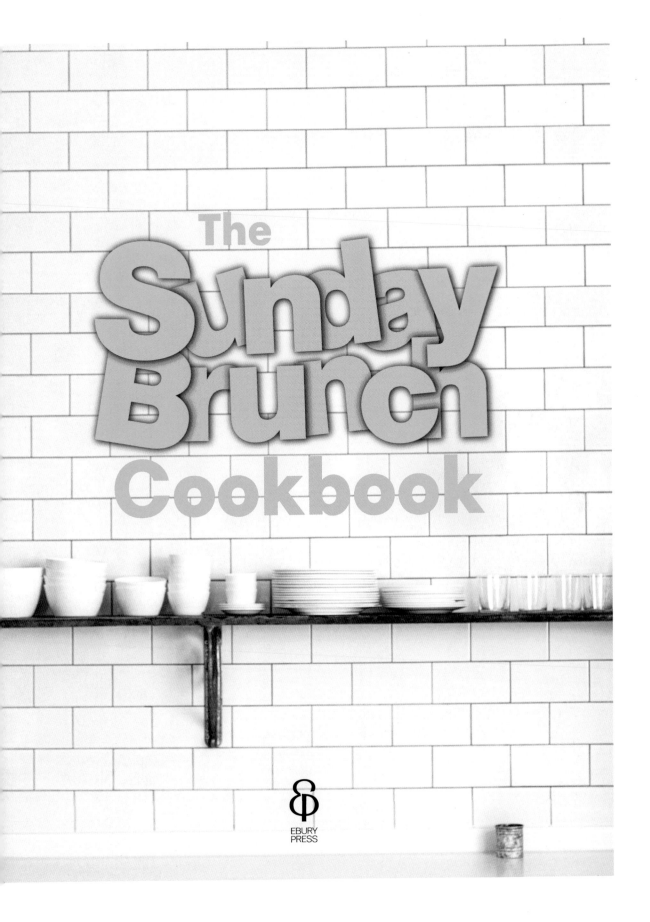

Hello and Welcome to
Sunday Brunch

We've been sitting alongside each other at *Sunday Brunch* 'school' for six years now. Each week the show starts in exactly the same way: our floor manager, Seb (the guy who laughs off-camera at our bad jokes), tells us there's one minute until we're on air, we then look at each other, realise that we don't know what we're doing and proceed to wing it for the next three hours.

Presenting *Sunday Brunch* is undoubtedly the best job in the world. We get to hang out with our mates. We cook great food. We sample fantastic drinks. We meet amazing guests and experts. Then, at the end of the show, we enjoy live music from top bands and artists, who perform whilst sitting on our sofas and standing on our rug.

Our single overriding aim is that we want to create recipes for everyone, dishes that we can all cook easily at home.

On each episode we cook three or four recipes with our guests for everyone to enjoy. A bit of basic maths tells us that, in the history of the show, we've cooked well over a thousand different dishes on TV. You might be able to imagine how tricky it was for us to whittle down all the recipes we've ever cooked onscreen to our top 100. However, there are some memorable dishes that stand out, and then there are those recipes that take on a life of their own and simply cannot be ignored.

More than anything else, we want the people sat at home watching us cook to think to themselves, 'Yep, I want to make that. I'm going to give it a go.' And now that we've collected our 100 best-ever recipes into this book, we hope even more of you feel inspired and encouraged to get into the kitchen.

Cooking on TV falls into one of two camps. The clever cheffy stuff – superb food, waaaaaay too tricky ever to attempt at home – or the 'I could do that' camp, which is where we sit. Simple, tasty food made from, in the main, easy-to-get-hold-of ingredients. For all our *Sunday Brunch* recipes, accessibility is key.

When writing recipes, we never forget that our viewers are going to see these dishes for the first time on a Sunday morning, perhaps when they're hungover or having a relaxing day on the sofa in front of the TV. So you want food that is simple, tasty, maybe with a bit of a twist (or 'Simon's drunken recipes', as Tim calls them) and, hopefully, something that becomes a firm family favourite.

The importance of ingredients is one of the very first things Simon taught Tim about good cooking. Pretty much all the ingredients used to make the recipes in this book can be picked up from a decent supermarket, and then for the odd piece of fish or cut of meat it really is worth seeking out a reliable fishmonger or butcher.

Picking up a few basic skills and an understanding of flavours, gives you the kitchen confidence to go on and experiment.

Tim here. Even though I've always enjoyed cooking, I'm the first to admit that, when I stepped into a kitchen together with Simon, I wasn't the most adventurous or most accomplished chef. But standing next to my mate each week and helping to cook such a variety of foods, I've taken away plenty of tips and techniques that I've translated into my own home cooking.

Nowadays, I would never dream of using a shop-bought jar of pasta sauce, tub of pesto or bottle of salad dressing as I've learnt just how easy it is to make all these things myself … and the taste of your own homemade version is incomparable.

When Simon plans a dish, he thinks about building layers of flavour, balancing acidity with the salty and the sweet, and incorporating contrasting textures. Combining a few key Asian ingredients, like soy sauce, fish sauce, rice vinegar, lime and honey into a marinade for fish and meat, understanding how to balance the acidity, heat, salt and sweetness, was my first step towards creating my now legendary Kung Fu Tuna (see page 96), which went on to produce the mantra, 'Be the Tuna'.

Simon here. I have been a chef for nearly 30 years, man and boy, but I am continually excited by food and by cooking. During our time on *Sunday Brunch*, the better cooking gospel according to Saint Simon has included:

1. Bring the meat or fish up to room temperature before cooking.
2. Oil the meat or fish and not the pan.
3. Don't shake mushrooms in the pan until you hear them squeak.
4. Everything tastes better when deep fried/with cheese/with chilli.
5. Butter and salt make things taste nice.
6. Cook out your tomato purée for 6–8 minutes before moving on.
7. Adding a teaspoon of vinegar at the end of cooking any non-cream based casserole is a winner (it opens your tastebuds).

Other nuggets I would add to this list are use the best produce you can, be patient, season carefully and taste as you go. And never get into a discussion with Tim about coriander.

Spices and herbs, along with garlic, salt and pepper, are so important. They are ingredients that do all the heavy lifting in the kitchen. By that we mean, it's these flavoursome fellas that really bring out the accents in our food. A handful of grassy parsley scattered over a plate or stirred through a stew at the end of the cooking really elevates a dish, brightening all the flavours. But we don't agree that every herb should be used so liberally. Anyone who has ever watched *Sunday Brunch* might just have picked up on the fact that Tim hates coriander. There's no persuading him. To Tim coriander is soapy poison. End of discussion.

Personal coriander preferences aside, food is a great leveller. Sharing a delicious meal is something that connects everyone, no matter who you are. We've had an incredibly varied range of guests cook with us in our studio kitchen. We've had knight of the realm Sir Ian McKellen pop on a *Sunday Brunch* apron to cook mackerel, we've had Hollywood legend and velvet-voiced chanteuse Kathleen Turner sizzle in the kitchen while cooking meatballs, and then we've had fictional telly pub landlord and all-round top geezer Danny Dyer – who could forget him 'folding the life' out of that cake mix. The best thing is when a guest gets stuck into the cooking – so much so that they forget whatever it is they've come on the show to promote.

We've seen some unorthodox cooking techniques over the episodes (we're looking at you, Richard Blackwood), but our advice to every home cook is to spend a bit of time learning how to chop correctly with the right knife. Learning how to hold a knife and slice an onion safely will stand you in good stead. Bearing in mind that pretty much every savoury dish starts with a chopped onion, it'll speed up your cooking. We use special celebrity onions that never make our guests' eyes water.

We're very lucky that the producers of *Sunday Brunch* don't set any parameters on the dishes that we cook with our guests each week. We've come to understand the type of food that not only pleases us, but that our guests and – more importantly – our viewers also love. The *Sunday Brunch* audience is our harshest critic but also our greatest inspiration. Please keep cooking our recipes. And please keep sharing photos of the dishes you cook from any of our recipes. If you make a recipe from this book, post it online with **#SundayBrunchCookbook** so that we can share in it too. And if you want to, go ahead and pose with the dish.

We really hope you like the top 100 of our super tasty, really easy, best-ever recipes. Ultimately, we just want to make food that people really want to cook for their tea.

morning!

Brunch is at the very heart of our show. It has to be, after all, it's in the title. Over the years we've probably cooked every possible brunch dish that there is, from savoury to sweet and sometimes a mix of both. In this chapter we've gathered together our favourite brunch dishes from over the years.

When enjoying a relaxed weekend brunch with family or friends, you don't want to be closeted in the kitchen. These recipes are all either quick to make, can be made ahead or will cook away in the oven while you mingle with your guests and maybe enjoy a drinkipoo.

Perhaps best of all, most of the brunch dishes in this chapter are made using just a single pan so there is very little kitchen carnage to be cleared away once the cooking is done.

Blueberry Pancakes with Eggs & Bacon

SERVES: **6**

200g self-raising flour
1 teaspoon bicarbonate of soda
50g caster sugar
1 egg, beaten
50g unsalted butter, melted
250ml whole milk
125g cottage cheese
225g blueberries, plus extra to serve
Sunflower oil, for frying
Black pepper

To serve
6 eggs
12 rashers of streaky bacon
15g unsalted butter
Maple syrup

This American-style stack of pancakes is served with maple bacon and topped with a perfectly poached egg. The occasional burst of blueberries in the pancakes provides a sharpness that cuts through the sweet syrup.

1. Combine the flour, bicarb and sugar together in a bowl.

2. In a separate bowl, combine the beaten egg, melted butter, milk and cottage cheese, then add this to the flour mix and stir to make a batter. Fold the blueberries into the batter

3. Warm a lightly oiled non-stick frying pan and, working in batches, spoon about 2 dessertspoons of batter per pancake into the pan. Cook for 1 minute on each side, or until golden.

4. Keep the pancakes warm while you poach the eggs (see page 18) and grill the bacon until very crispy.

5. Serve the pancakes in stacks, with a dab of butter and some bacon between each layer. Top with an egg, grind over some pepper then drizzle over maple syrup and serve with extra blueberries.

Perfectly Poached Eggs

1 egg per person (or more if
you're especially hungry)
Splash of white wine vinegar

TOP TIP

*For a perfectly shaped egg with no wispy bits,
first line a teacup or ramekin with clingfilm,
crack the egg into the clingfilm and then tightly
twist the clingfilm together at the top into a
parcel, making sure there is no air trapped
inside. Place the parcel in the pan of simmering
water and poach the egg inside the clingfilm.
When ready, remove the parcel from the pan,
unwrap the egg and discard the clingfilm.
You'll be left with a neat, smooth, spherical
poached egg.*

Eggs are the original fast food – versatile, inexpensive and a great source of protein in the morning to fuel you for the day ahead. A poached egg on its own makes a simple meal, but something simple done well is a beautiful thing. Adding a poached egg to a dish, from blueberry pancakes to duck hash and even beans on toast, can take a meal from the average to the sublime.

1. Bring a large pan of water to a simmer. Add a splash of white wine vinegar to the simmering water. Do not add salt to the water at this stage.

2. Crack the egg into a teacup or ramekin, taking care not to break the yolk.

3. Stir the water with a wooden spoon to create a vortex in the pan – this helps the egg to hold its shape.

4. Slowly tip the egg into the swirling water.

5. Simmer (rather than boil) the egg. Cook it for 3 minutes for an oozy, runny yolk or 4 minutes if you prefer the yolk a little firmer.

6. Once cooked, remove the egg from the pan using a slotted spoon. Set aside on paper towels to absorb any excess moisture.

Filthy Dirty
Ham & Cheese Toastie

MAKES: **1**

2 slices of white bread, cut 2cm thick
60g unsalted butter, melted
1 teaspoon Dijon mustard
50g roast ham, thickly sliced
50g mature Cheddar, grated
25g mozzarella, grated
10g Parmesan, finely grated
2 tablespoons maple syrup,
plus extra to serve

A ham and cheese toastie is always a winning brunch, but take it to the next level by finishing it in the pan with a generous drizzle of maple syrup. Allow the syrup to caramelise and reach a deep brown colour. This is a dish to eat naked.

1. Brush one side of each slice of bread with half the melted butter.

2. Fry the bread, buttered side down, in a frying pan over a medium heat for 4 minutes, or until golden. Transfer to a plate.

3. Spread the mustard on the toasted side of one slice of bread, then lay the ham over the mustard, followed by the grated cheeses.

4. Sit the other slice of bread, uncooked side up, on top. Press down gently.

5. Heat the remaining butter in the frying pan. As the butter foams, add the sandwich and cook for 2 minutes.

6. Add the maple syrup to the pan and increase the heat. Flip the sandwich over and cook on the other side for a further 2 minutes.

7. Remove the toastie from the pan, cut it in half then return it to the pan, cut side down, to caramelise. Serve immediately with extra maple syrup.

Duck Hash

SERVES: **6**

4 duck legs
125ml olive oil, plus extra for the onion
1 cinnamon stick
2 garlic cloves
1 onion, sliced
2 baking potatoes, peeled, coarsely grated and any water squeezed out
1 teaspoon chilli flakes
100g unsalted butter
4 gherkins, sliced
1 tablespoon chopped parsley
Salt and black pepper

To serve
Slices of sourdough toast
6 poached eggs (see page 18 for method)
Chilli sauce

Nowadays, anything goes on toast. Duck is a beautifully rich meat, that is criminally underused when it comes to brunch dishes. That is all about to change. Rather than compact the duck hash into cakes, here the meat is shredded and then folded together with the potatoes and gerkins before serving on sourdough toast.

1. Preheat the oven to 160°C fan/180°C/Gas 4.

2. Place the duck legs in a roasting tray and pour over the olive oil. Add the cinnamon stick and garlic to the tray, season well, cover and roast for about 40 minutes.

3. Remove and leave to cool. When cool enough to handle, shred all the meat from the bones, and discard the cinnamon and garlic.

4. Fry the onion for 10 minutes in oil until soft and beginning to caramelise.

5. Add the grated potato, chilli flakes and butter to the pan, then cook over a medium heat, stirring occasionally, for about 8 minutes until the potato is cooked and crisp.

6. Fold in the shredded duck meat, gherkins and parsley.

7. Serve on slices of toast, topped with a poached egg and a drizzle of chilli sauce.

Chorizo Breakfast Burrito

SERVES: **6**

200g cooking chorizo, chopped
A little oil
6 eggs
6 tablespoons whole milk
1 tablespoon unsalted butter
3 roasted red peppers (from a jar)
Handful of baby spinach
1 red chilli, finely chopped
6 soft corn tortillas (flour tortillas will do if you can't find corn ones), warmed
200g Manchego cheese, grated
Salt and black pepper

To serve
Hot sauce
Sour cream

Wake up your tastebuds with these breakfast burritos. The smokiness and heat of the chorizo, peppers and chillis are contrasted by the buttery soft scrambled eggs and cooling sour cream.

1. Fry the chorizo in oil in a large frying pan until a little crisp, remove from the pan and set aside. Don't clean out the pan as the oil from the chorizo will be used later.

2. Beat the eggs in a bowl, then add the milk and some seasoning.

3. Melt the butter in the pan used to fry the chorizo. As it begins to foam, add the eggs, then add the chorizo back in and leave to cook until the egg starts to set, without disturbing it.

4. Once it starts to set, move the egg gently towards the centre, using a spatula, until it's just set, then flip over and take off the heat.

5. Roughly chop the peppers with the spinach and add to the egg pan, along with the chilli. (The spinach will wilt down in the pan's heat.)

6. Place a line of pepper, spinach and egg mixture just off centre down the middle of each tortilla, then sprinkle grated cheese down the side.

7. Roll up tightly and serve with hot sauce and sour cream.

Coconut Pancakes with Prawns, Beansprouts & Pepper

SERVES: **4**

100g rice flour
1 teaspoon ground turmeric
60ml coconut milk
150ml ice-cold sparkling water
2 spring onions, finely chopped
Vegetable oil, for frying

For the filling
250g raw king prawns, peeled and deveined
100g beansprouts, washed
1 red pepper, finely sliced
Half gem lettuce, shredded
Handful of mint or coriander leaves, shredded
100g salted peanuts, crushed

For the dressing
3 tablespoons fish sauce
3 tablespoons lime juice
3 tablespoons light soy
2 teaspoons sugar
1 bird's eye chilli, finely chopped

These Vietnamese-inspired crispy coconut pancakes combine so well with the sweet prawns, crunchy beansprouts and fragrant herbs to create a brunch dish with a difference.

1. Combine the flour and turmeric together in a bowl. Briefly whisk the coconut milk, then add to the flour with the ice-cold water. Whisk everything together to make a smooth batter. Add the spring onions and season with salt and pepper. Leave the batter to rest for 30 minutes.

2. To make the dressing, whisk together the fish sauce, lime juice and light soy with 1½ tablespoons cold water in a bowl. Add the sugar and stir until it has dissolved. Add the chopped chilli and then set aside.

3. Heat about 1 tablespoon of oil in a frying pan, and pour a quarter of the pancake batter into the pan. Cook for 2–3 minutes until the pancake is cooked through. There is no need to flip the pancake over. Transfer to a plate and repeat until all the batter has been used up. Keep the pancakes warm.

4. To make the filling, heat about 1 tablespoon oil in a wok or large frying pan, add the prawns and cook until they just turn pink. Add the beansprouts and red pepper and cook for another minute. Next, add the shredded lettuce, herbs and peanuts, mix well and cook for a final minute.

5. Place a quarter of the prawn, beansprout and pepper mixture on one half of each pancake, then fold over. Serve with lime wedges.

Courgette Fritters with Tomato & Avocado Salsa

SERVES: **4**

For the pancakes
2 courgettes, finely grated
1 teaspoon chilli flakes
1 teaspoon smoked paprika
2 spring onions, chopped
Handful of mint leaves, chopped
200g gram flour, sifted
Vegetable oil, for frying
Salt and black pepper

For the salsa
200g cherry tomatoes, quartered or chopped
1 avocado, diced
1 red chilli, finely sliced
½ cucumber, diced
Grated zest and juice of 2 limes
Handful of coriander leaves, chopped

To serve
Feta, finely crumbled

These veg-packed pancakes make a fantastically hearty meat-free brunch. The moisture in the courgettes means that you only need to add a small amount of water to make the batter.

1. To make the salsa, simply mix the tomatoes, avocado, chilli and cucumber together in a bowl. Season well and add the lime zest and juice, then scatter over the chopped coriander.

2. Mix the grated courgette, chilli flakes, smoked paprika, spring onions, mint and gram flour in a bowl with plenty of salt and pepper. Stir in just enough cold water (approximately 50ml) to make a thick batter.

3. Heat about a 1cm depth of oil in a frying pan, and dollop spoonfuls of the pancake mixture into the pan. Flatten them out with a spoon and cook for 3 minutes on each side.

4. To serve, stack the pancakes on plates, spoon over some of the salsa, then crumble over the feta.

Salmon & Egg Brunch Pies

SERVES: **4**

For the pastry
450g plain flour, plus extra for dusting
50ml whole milk
50ml water
150g lard, chopped
1 egg yolk, beaten
Salt and black pepper

For the filling
5 hard-boiled eggs, chopped
1 tablespoon capers
200g smoked salmon, chopped
200g cooked new potatoes, chopped
1 tablespoon chopped dill
1 tablespoon sour cream
Grated zest of 1 lemon

To serve
75g mayonnaise
2 teaspoons wholegrain mustard
Mixed salad leaves

These tasty brunch pies are made using hot-water pastry, which is really robust. Due to its lard content, hot-water pastry can withstand both high temperatures and long cooking times, so it's perfect for pies. This is the SAS of pastry as it can contain any situation.

You will need 4 small loose-bottomed pork pie tins.

1. To make the hot-water pastry, sift the flour into a mixing bowl and season well with salt and pepper.

2. Place the milk, water and lard in a pan and place over a low heat until the lard has melted.

3. Bring just to the boil and pour onto the flour mix, stir well, then turn onto a floured surface and knead for 3–4 minutes.

4. Divide the pastry into four equal portions. From each portion, save enough pastry for a lid, then roll the remaining dough out into a rough circle. (If this proves too difficult to do, press the pastry straight into the tin.) Press the rolled-out pastry rounds into the four small pork pie tins, making sure that you have some pastry overhanging the edges.

Continued overleaf →

*Instead of using salmon in the pie filling,
you can substitute another oily fish,
such as smoked trout or mackerel.*

*These pies can be made and chilled the day
before, ready to be baked the next day.*

5. Work the pastry up the sides to make it even, using your hands, then use a bottle – something like a Worcestershire sauce bottle is the perfect size – as you would a rolling pin, to give a smooth finish to the pastry.

6. Roll out the reserved pastry to make lids for the pies. Cut the pastry lids to the size of the inside of the tin.

7. For the filling, combine all the ingredients and season well, then divide between the pastry-lined tins. Make sure there is a small raised mound of filling in the centre at the top of each pie.

8. Brush a little egg wash over the rims of the pie sides then place the lids on top, fold the edges over onto the lid in towards the centre. Use the tip of a kitchen knife to gently press around the edges to seal well.

9. Place the pies in the fridge to chill, and preheat the oven to 160°C fan/180°C/Gas 4.

10. Brush all over the pie lid with more egg wash and use the knife tip to create a steam hole in the centre. Bake for 45 minutes or until the pastry is light golden.

11. Remove from the oven and allow the pies to cool in the tins. When completely cool, remove from the tins.

12. Mix the mayonnaise with the mustard, then serve the pies with a few salad leaves and a dollop of mustard mayo.

Spicy Bombay Potato Rolls

Flaky filo pastry wrapped around a beautiful spiced potato filling is one cracking way to start the day.

1. Gently fry the onion and garlic for about 15 minutes, or until soft and caramelised.

2. Add the spuds and spices, cook for about 8 minutes over med-high heat to get some colour on the spuds.

3. Add the tomatoes and coriander, take off the heat. Allow to cool completely.

4. When ready to make the rolls, pour the vegetable oil into a bowl and stir in the ground turmeric. Lay a sheet of filo pastry on a clean, flat work surface. Brush the filo with oil, then layer another sheet of filo on top. Brush more oil onto the pastry and add a third sheet of filo.

5. Place a quarter of the spicy potato mixture on top of the filo pastry, laying it diagonally in line from corner to corner.

6. Roll up tightly, folding in the edges of the pastry to enclose the filling in neat parcels. Repeat with the rest of the pastry sheets and filling to make four rolls.

7. Brush the outside of the pastry rolls with more of the oil. Bake at 180°C fan/200°C/Gas 6 for about 25–30 minutes, or until golden.

8. Blend the mint, coriander, vinegar and sugar in a small bowl. Serve as a dipping sauce alongside the hot rolls.

SERVES: **4**

200ml vegetable oil
2 teaspoons ground turmeric
12 sheets of filo pastry, approximately 23cm square

For the filling
2 onions, finely sliced
2 garlic cloves, finely sliced
225g cubed, blanched potatoes
½ teaspoon chilli flakes
1 teaspoon each of ground cumin, coriander, ginger, turmeric and garam masala
3 tomatoes, deseeded and chopped
Handful coriander leaves, chopped

For the dipping sauce
250g mint leaves, chopped
100g coriander, chopped
3 tablespoons white wine vinegar
2 teaspoons sugar

Beans on Toast

Yes, you can easily open a tin of baked beans and make yourself an almost instant breakfast, but they won't be a patch on these creamy butter beans simmered in a rich tomato sauce. When we cooked this on the show, this was one of those recipes where Tim reckoned that Simon was 'getting away with it'. That was, until he tucked in ...

1. Gently fry the onion and garlic in oil in a pan for about 15 minutes, or until soft and caramelised.

2. Add the tomatoe purée to the pan and continue to cook, stirring, for 6 minutes.

3. Add the red wine to the pan, increase the heat and boil until the wine is reduced by half.

4. Add the vegetable stock and plum tomatoes to the pan, reduce the heat to low and simmer for 10 minutes.

5. Add the butter beans to the tomato sauce and simmer for 5 minutes, stirring occasionally.

6. Finally, stir in the butter and olive oil until everything is well combined.

7. Serve on slices of hot buttered sourdough toast, topped with a perect poached egg.

SERVES: **4**

For the beans
1 onion, finely sliced
1 garlic clove, crushed
2 tablespoons olive oil
2 tablespoons tomato purée
100ml red wine
100ml vegetable stock
1 x 400g tin of skinned, chopped plum tomatoes
2 x 400g tins of butter beans, rinsed and drained
25g unsalted butter
75ml extra virgin olive oil

To serve
Slices of sourdough toast, buttered
4 poached eggs (see page 18 for method)

Shakshuka Eggs with Feta

SERVES: **4-6**

2 tablespoons olive oil
1 red onion, thinly sliced
3 garlic cloves, thinly sliced
1 red pepper, thinly sliced
2 x 400g tins of chopped tomatoes
1 teaspoon ground cumin
1 teaspoon smoked sweet paprika
½ teaspoon cayenne pepper
150g feta, crumbled
6 eggs
A few coriander leaves
Salt and black pepper

To serve
Slices of sourdough toast
Hot sauce

This brilliant one-pan brunch dish is a guaranteed crowdpleaser. Carry the pan to the brunch table and encourage your guests to tuck in. An added bonus is the minimal clearing up once brunch has been eaten.

1. Preheat the oven to 160°C fan/180°C/Gas 4.

2. Heat the oil in a flameproof dish or ovenproof frying pan, add the onion, garlic and pepper and gently fry for about 15 minutes, until just caramelised.

3. Add the tomatoes, spices and some salt and pepper, and cook for 10 minutes.

4. Scatter over the crumbled feta. Make 6 small wells in the tomato mixture, crack an egg into each well and bake in the oven for 10–12 minutes, or until the eggs are set.

5. Top with the coriander leaves and serve with slices of toasted sourdough and hot sauce.

Indian Spiced Potato
& Eggs

SERVES: **4-6**

3 tablespoons butter
1 onion, finely diced
2 garlic cloves, crushed
200g new potatoes, boiled and roughly chopped
1 red chilli, finely chopped
1 teaspoon each of ground cumin and turmeric
2 teaspoons medium curry powder
2 tomatoes, deseeded and finely chopped
75g frozen peas
6 eggs
50ml double cream
1 tablespoon chopped coriander

To serve
Chapatis

These softly scrambled eggs should be cooked gently over a medium heat, rather than fast and furious over a high heat. Go slow. Take your time. No one enjoys rubbery eggs.

1. Melt the butter in a wide pan or frying pan and gently fry the onion and garlic until soft.

2. Add the potatoes, chilli and dry spices and cook for 4 minutes. Add the tomatoes and cook for 3 minutes, then add the frozen peas.

3. Beat the eggs and cream together, add to the pan and stir constantly until just holding their form, about 6–8 minutes.

4. Scatter over the coriander and serve with warm chapatis.

Mexican Smashed Avocado on Toast

SERVES: **6**

4 avocados
2 plum tomatoes, deseeded and diced
¼ red onion, finely diced
2 red chillies, finely chopped
½ bunch of coriander, stems chopped and
leaves reserved
Grated zest and juice of 3 limes
200g feta
Handful of chopped mint
6 thick slices of sourdough, toasted or griddled
Salt and black pepper

To serve
Hot sauce

STONING AN AVOCADO

Sometimes a guest blows us away with their surprise kitchen skills. Singer-songwriter Jason Mraz – who happens to own an avocado farm in San Diego – managed to stone an avocado in record time. Here's how to do it safely … Place the avocado on a chopping board. Using a sharp knife, run the blade through the skin and flesh, from the tip of the fruit to the base and then up the other side back to the tip. Holding one half of the avocado in each hand, twist in opposite directions to separate. One half will have the stone still in it. With just enough force to pierce the stone, tap the heel of the knife into the stone and twist to remove.

The entire world seems to be in the grip of an avocado obsession. Even if you feel that we've reached Peak Avocado, we urge you to try this Mexican-inspired version of avo toast. The chunks of creamy green fruit are enlivened by the zing of red onion, chilli and lime and the delicious saltiness of the feta. Tim says that the coriander should be optional.

1. Peel and stone the avocados, then scoop the flesh into a large bowl.

2. Add the tomatoes, onion, chillies, coriander stems and lime zest and juice to the avocados.

3. Using a fork, break down the avocados until the flesh is in bite-sized chunks. Season to taste with salt and pepper.

4. Crumble the feta into another bowl and mix with the chopped mint and more lime juice.

5. Spoon the smashed avocado mixture onto the slices of toast.

6. Crumble the feta over the top, scatter with the reserved coriander leaves, and serve with hot sauce on the side.

South of the Border
Eggs Benedict

Within the Brunch Premiership, the breakfast classic Eggs Benedict has to be top of the league. This southern-style version of 'Eggs Benny', with a piquant sauce smothered over oozy poached eggs and crispy fried potatoes, brings the tastebud-tingling flair of a Champions League winner.

1. Blanch the diced potatoes in a pan of boiling water for 8 minutes, then drain. Heat some oil in a frying pan, add the spuds, chilli and garlic, then cook on high heat for 3 minutes, or until everything begins to crisp up.

SERVES: **4**

2-3 tablespoons vegetable oil
450g potatoes, peeled and diced
1 red chilli, finely chopped
1 garlic clove, finely chopped
150g unsalted butter, diced
Grated zest and juice of 1 lime
Handful of chopped coriander
8 poached eggs (see page 18 for method)
Salt and black pepper

For the sauce
2 egg yolks
½ teaspoon white wine vinegar
1 tablespoon ice-cold water
125g clarified butter
Juice of ½ lemon
1 tablespoon chipotle hot sauce

2. Add the butter and lime zest, then cook for a further 4 minutes.

3. Add the lime juice and season well with salt and pepper. Drain off any excess oil, then add the chopped coriander.

4. To make the sauce, put the egg yolks, vinegar and water in a heatproof bowl and whisk together using a balloon whisk, to combine.

5. Put the bowl over a pan of barely simmering water and whisk for 4 minutes. Take off the heat and slowly whisk in the clarified butter until nice and thick. Stir in the lemon juice and chipotle sauce.

6. Serve the crispy fried spuds with 2 poached eggs per person and a good dollop of the sauce.

Granola with Coconut & Maple Syrup

MAKES: **1 LARGE JAR**

For the granola
200g rolled oats
50g hazelnuts, chopped
25g pecans, chopped
25g golden raisins
15g desiccated coconut
50g demerara sugar
175ml maple syrup
50g coconut oil, melted

SERVES: **4**

For the fruit
2 bananas, sliced
100g blueberries
1 mango, chopped
Grated zest and juice of 1 lime
1 tablespoon maple syrup

To serve
Coconut or soya yoghurt

Granola is so simple to create at home, and the beauty of making it yourself is that you can tailor the combination of ingredients to include your favourite dried fruit and nuts. Using coconut oil to bind the ingredients together in clusters not only gives the granola a gorgeously nutty taste, but it also means that this version is vegan friendly and so can be enjoyed by everyone. This recipe makes more granola than you will need for four servings, so store what's left over for up to two weeks in an airtight container.

1. Preheat the oven to 130°C fan/150°C/Gas 2.

2. Mix all the ingredients for the granola together and spread out on a baking tray. Roast for about 15 minutes, or until rich golden brown. Set aside to cool completely.

3. Combine the ingredients for the fruit.

4. Serve a pool of yoghurt in a shallow bowl topped with the granola and mixed fruits.

Images overleaf →

Brioche French Toast with Honey-Glazed Nectarines

SERVES: **4**

2 eggs
250ml whole milk
1 teaspoon vanilla paste
1 tablespoon honey, plus extra to serve
1 teaspoon ground cinnamon
4 thick slices of brioche
About 100g unsalted butter, for frying

For the roasted hazelnuts
150g hazelnuts
25ml vegetable or sunflower oil

For the nectarines
3 nectarines, sliced
Grated zest of 1 orange
3 tablespoons honey

To serve
Greek yoghurt
Honey

This brioche French toast served with warm, honey-glazed nectarines is a posh version of the eggy bread we enjoyed as kids. The vanilla and cinnamon add a lovely warmth that contrasts the sharpess of the stone fruit, while the roasted hazelnuts add a satisfying crunch.

1. Preheat the oven to 160°C fan/180°C/Gas 4.

2. To roast the hazelnuts, toss them in the oil, spread out on a baking tray and roast in the hot oven for about 12 minutes, giving them the odd shake from time to time. Remove from the oven and allow to cool. When cool enough to handle, roughly chop the hazelnuts.

3. In the meantime, place the nectarine slices in a frying pan with the orange zest and honey. Cook gently, turning them, for about 5 minutes or until soft and sticky.

4. In a shallow bowl, beat the eggs with the milk, vanilla paste, honey and cinnamon.

5. Dip the brioche slices in the beaten egg mixture. Melt the butter in a frying pan and fry each brioche slice for 2–3 minutes on each side. Don't shake the pan or fiddle with the bread, as you want it to caramelise in the pan.

6. Serve the French toast topped with the honey-glazed nectarines, chopped hazelnuts, Greek yoghurt and more honey.

Whether it's a refreshing juice blend, kickstarter
shot of coffee or a restorative hair-of-the dog, there's
a brunch-time drink to suit everyone. Cheers!

Ian Burrell's Strong Back

SERVES: **1**

100ml Guinness
25ml Jamaican rum
50ml condensed milk
Pinch of nutmeg

1. Fill a tall highball glass with ice and pour the Guinness and rum into the glass over the ice.

2. Add the condensed milk and nutmeg to the glass and stir to mix well until the condensed milk has dissolved.

Karina Elias's Nordic Spark

SERVES: **1**

45ml Aquavit
45ml Cocchi
A dash of Angostura bitters
A dash of absinthe
Champagne, to top up
A strip of lemon peel, to garnish

1. Pour the Aquavit and Cocchi into a cocktail shaker. Dash in the Angostura bitters and absinthe, then shake the cocktail shaker vigorously.

2. Fill a tall Collins glass with ice. Strain the contents of the shaker into the glass over the ice.

3. Top up the glass with Champagne.

4. Garnish with a strip of lemon peel.

Carl Brown's Lemon & Lime Bitters

SERVES: 1

For the home-made lemonade
A pinch of sea salt
25ml freshly squeezed lemon juice
10ml sugar syrup
15ml lime cordial (such as Roses)

For the cocktail
Lemonade mix (see above)
35ml gin
4 dashes of Angostura bitters
Soda, to top up
Lemon and limes slices, to garnish

1. To make the home-made lemonade, combine all the ingredients in a jug and stir to mix.

2. To make the cocktail, fill a tall highball glass with ice and pour the lemonade mix and gin into the glass over the ice.

3. Dash in the Angostura bitters and then top up the glass with soda.

4. Garnish with slices of lemon and lime.

Neil Ridley & Joel Harrison's Bloody Maria

SERVES: 1

50ml tequila (such as Jose Cuervo
   Tradicional Silver Tequila)
100ml tomato juice (for an extra fresh hit,
   use a cold-pressed juice)
3 dashes of Cholula chipotle hot sauce
2½ teaspoons freshly squeezed lime juice
A dash of Worcester sauce
½ teaspoon celery salt
½ teaspoon freshly ground black pepper
Lime wedge, to garnish
Celery stick, to garnish

1. Fill a tall highball glass with ice, then pour the tequila and tomato into the glass over the ice.

2. Add the hot sauce and lime juice to the glass. Dash in the Worcester sauce, then add the celery salt and black pepper and stir to mix well.

3. Garnish with a lime wedge and a celery stick.

small,
but perfect

At Sunday Brunch we don't really do dainty canapés. That isn't exactly our style. We prefer something a bit more substantial. Instead, the recipes gathered in this chapter are more small plates that – despite their size – pack a full-on flavour punch.

Cook one of these small, but perfect dishes to make a light supper for a few friends, to serve as a starter during a multi-course meal or, for a larger gathering, prepare a selection of small plates and encourage everyone to try a bit of each. As the saying goes, good things do come in small packages.

Chorizo & Cheese Sausage Roll

MAKES: **4**

175g cooking chorizo, cut into small pieces
(or buy pre-diced to save time)
2 tablespoons dry sherry
400g sausage meat
100g Manchego cheese, grated
1 tablespoon chopped parsley
1 x 500g block of puff pastry
1 egg yolk, lightly beaten
Salt and black pepper

To serve
Chilli sauce, tomato ketchup or
tomato chutney

The sausage roll is a staple of every buffet table. Done well it is a thing of beauty. Our version embraces the Spanish flavours of smoky, spicy chorizo and buttery Manchego cheese, made from sheep's milk. if you can't find Manchego, you can always substitute Gruyère cheese. Life is definitely too short to make your own puff pastry from scratch. Buy a block of readymade puff from your local supermarket. We won't judge.

1. Preheat the oven to 180°C fan/200°C/Gas 6. Line a baking tray with baking parchment.

2. In a non-stick frying pan, fry the chorizo until crispy. (As the chorizo is oily, you won't need to add any extra oil to the pan.)

3. Add the sherry to the chorizo in the pan, then reduce to nearly nothing.

4. Tip the chorizo into a bowl with the sausage meat, cheese and parsley. Season and mix well.

Continued overleaf →

When handling the puff pastry, make sure your hands are nice and cold. If they're too warm while you're working the dough, the butter or fat in the pastry might start to melt before it reaches the oven and you won't get such good flakes. You can always chill the prepared sausage rolls in the fridge for 15 minutes before baking to keep their shape firm.

5. Roll out the pastry on a lightly floured surface to a 30cm square, then cut into four equal 15cm squares.

6. Divide the sausage mixture between the pastry squares, placing it in a long strip down the middle of each square.

7. Roll each into a cylinder, trim the excess wrap-over of pastry, creating a seam. Lightly press the seam together to seal and place seam-side down on the lined baking tray.

8. Brush with egg yolk and bake for about 20 minutes, or until the pastry is puffed, crispy and deep golden.

9. Serve with your favourite accompaniments.

Roasted Radish with Creamy Feta & Pickled Walnuts

SERVES: **4-6**

250g radishes, halved
30ml olive oil
6 pickled walnuts, sliced
1 tablespoon nigella seeds
Handful of rocket leaves (optional)
Sea salt and black pepper

For the creamy feta
150g feta
30g Greek yoghurt
30ml extra virgin olive oil, plus extra to serve
Grated zest and juice of ½ lemon

To serve
Warm pitta

Crumbled, mashed or whipped, feta is one of our favourite cheeses. Roasted radishes and pickled walnuts might seem like old-school ingredients from your nanna's pantry, but do try this winning combo.

1. Preheat the oven to 160°C fan/180°C/Gas 4.

2. Toss the halved radishes in the oil and season with salt and pepper, then spread out on a roasting tray and roast for 10–12 minutes. You don't want them to char, just to warm through and keep their colour – if you cook them for too long, they lose their pink hue and go an unattractive grey.

3. Meanwhile, place the feta in a bowl with the yoghurt, oil and lemon zest and juice. Mash with a fork until spreadable but not completely smooth.

4. Spread the feta over a round serving plate, drizzle with extra virgin olive oil, then arrange the warm radishes and the pickled walnut slices on top.

5. Sprinkle over the nigella seeds, add rocket leaves if you like, then dig in with the warm pitta.

Images overleaf →

Gougères with Bacon & Mustard Dip

Small savoury cheese puffs of choux pastry, gougères are delicious on their own, but they're out of this world when dipped into this bacon and mustard mayo.

1. Preheat the oven to 160°C fan/180°C/Gas 4. Grease 2 baking trays and line with baking parchment.

2. Put the water, milk, butter and salt in a pan and bring to the boil.

3. Add the flour, beat well, then cook for 2 minutes.

4. Transfer to a bowl, cool for 1 minute then beat in the eggs, one at a time.

5. Stir in the grated cheese and nutmeg.

6. Put the mixture into a piping bag and pipe small balls, about the size of a golf ball, onto the prepared baking trays.

7. Sprinkle some grated cheese on top and bake for about 25 minutes, until cooked through and golden brown.

8. For the dipping sauce, grill the bacon until very crispy. Finely chop all but a couple of rashers and mix with the remaining ingredients in a bowl. Break the reserved bacon into pieces and add to the top of the dipping sauce. Serve the gougères with the dipping sauce, and some rocket if you like.

SERVES: **4-6**

125ml water
125ml milk
100g butter, plus extra for greasing
1 teaspoon sea salt
125g plain flour
4 medium eggs
75g Gruyère, grated, plus 25g extra to sprinkle on top
1 teaspoon freshly grated nutmeg

For the dipping sauce
100g smoked streaky bacon
125g mayonnaise
75g crème fraîche
30g Dijon mustard
1 teaspoon smoked paprika

Jalapeño Cheese Poppers

Creamy, cheesy deep-fried poppers make the perfect party food. They're guaranteed to disappear in minutes.

1. Combine the cream cheese, jalapeños and coriander, with salt to taste, then chill in the fridge for 1 hour.

2. Roll the chilled mixture into balls, each weighing about 25g.

3. Put the flour, eggs, polenta and breadcrumbs into 4 separate dishes or shallow bowls. Coat each chilled ball first in the flour, then in the beaten egg, then the polenta. Dip each again in the egg and then in the breadcrumbs to coat all over.

4. Pour enough oil for deep-frying into a deep-fryer or wide, deep pan, making sure it is no more than one-third full. Heat to 180°C, or until a cube of white bread browns in just under 1 minute.

5. Carefully lower the poppers into the oil in batches and deep-fry for 2–3 minutes, or until lightly golden.

6. Serve with the tomato and avocado salsa and Parmesan shavings.

SERVES: **4-6**

250g cream cheese
125g jalapeños, drained, chopped and patted dry
25g coriander leaves, chopped
50g plain flour
2 medium eggs, beaten
75g polenta
75g breadcrumbs
Vegetable oil, for deep-frying
Generous pinch of salt

To serve
Tomato and avocado salsa (see page 27)
Parmesan shavings

Thai Chicken Meatballs with Nuoc Cham Dipping Sauce

SERVES: **4-6**

For the meatballs
300g chicken mince
50g red Thai curry paste
2 tablespoons fish sauce
1 teaspoon sugar
3 lime leaves, shredded
20g coriander leaves, chopped
10 fine green beans, finely chopped
1 lemongrass stalk, very finely chopped
2 tablespoons sesame seeds
1 egg

For the dipping sauce
75ml light soy sauce
100g mayonnaise
Grated zest and juice of 1 lime
1 red chilli, finely chopped
2 tablespoons chopped coriander

Vegetable or sunflower oil, for frying
Limes wedges, to serve

All the best Asian flavours are rolled into this single dish, with the citrus tang of lemongrass and the umami savoury depth of fish sauce in these Thai-inspired chicken meatballs.

1. Mix all the meatball ingredients together well, then mould into 4cm balls. Chill for at least 40 minutes.

2. Heat enough oil for shallow-frying in a frying pan over a medium heat and fry the meatballs for about 8–10 minutes, turning them, until cooked through. (Alternatively, you can brown them quickly and finish them in a 180°C fan/ 200°C/Gas 6 oven to cook through.)

3. For the dipping sauce, combine all the ingredients together in a small bowl.

4. Serve the meatballs with the dipping sauce and lime wedges to squeeze over.

Sausage Stuffed Red Onions

SERVES: **4-6**

6 small or 4 larger red onions
2 garlic cloves, sliced
30ml olive oil
150ml water
250g pork sausage meat
1 teaspoon fennel seeds, crushed
1 teaspoon chilli flakes
250ml double cream
1 bay leaf
Salt and black pepper

To serve
Crusty bread

More of a satisfying lunch than a dainty fingerfood, these sausage-stuffed onions pack a mighty flavour punch with the aniseed of the fennel seeds and the warmth of the chilli flakes.

1. Preheat the oven to 160°C fan/180°C/Gas 4.

2. Slice the top off each red onion and peel them, leaving the stem end intact. Put into a roasting tin.

3. Take out the core of each onion to make a cavity, then push a little garlic inside each. Season well and drizzle over the oil. Add the water to the tin, around the onions.

4. Cover in foil and bake for about 50 minutes, then remove the onions from the tin and leave to cool.

5. Remove the middle few layers from each onion and set aside.

6. Mix the sausage meat with the fennel seeds and chilli flakes, and season well.

7. Stuff the sausage meat mixture into the onions, filling them generously so that the mixture spills out of the top of the onion.

8. Put the cream, reserved onion middles and bay leaf into the roasting tin and boil on the hob for 5 minutes.

9. Add the onions back to the tin and roast in the oven for 25 minutes. Serve with crusty bread.

Tuscan-Style Chicken Livers on Toast

We cooked these Tuscan-style chicken livers when Stanley Tucci joined us on the show. That's Stanley Tucci the Italian-American Oscar-nominated actor who has also written a couple of bestselling cookbooks... so, you know, no pressure!

1. Put the oil and butter in a frying pan and gently heat until the butter has melted. Add the shallots, garlic, anchovies, capers and sage leaves and gently fry for 6 minutes. Remove from the pan.

2. Add the livers and cook for 4 minutes on each side, or until golden.

3. Add half the wine and return the aromatics to the pan. Cook, beginning to break the livers down with a wooden spoon, until all the wine is absorbed.

4. Add the rest of the wine and repeat. Take off the heat and allow to cool a little.

5. Transfer the mixture to a food processor, add the lemon zest and Parmesan and pulse to your preferred consistency.

6. Season with salt and pepper to taste and spread on slices of toast just before serving, topped with a dollop of your favourite chutney and a few rocket leaves.

SERVES: **4-6**

30ml olive oil
50g butter
2 banana shallots, finely sliced
2 garlic cloves, finely chopped
3 salted anchovies, chopped
15g capers, chopped
6 sage leaves
600g chicken livers, trimmed and patted dry (450g prepared weight)
160ml dry white wine
Grated zest of ½ lemon
55g Parmesan, finely grated
Salt and black pepper

To serve
Slices of toast
Chutney
Rocket leaves

Salt Cod Fritters
with Garlic Aïoli

SERVES: **4-6**

750g wet salt cod, well rinsed
60g plain flour
1 teaspoon dried yeast
1 egg
2–3 tablespoons honey, plus extra to serve
60ml ice-cold water
Vegetable oil, for frying

For the aïoli
1 egg yolk
1 teaspoon Dijon mustard
500ml extra virgin olive oil
1 garlic clove, crushed
Grated zest and juice of 1 lemon
Sea salt and black pepper

To serve
Rocket leaves

Dried, salted cod must be re-hydrated before use, so leave enough time to soak it before use.

1. First make the aïoli. In a small mixing bowl, beat the egg yolk together with the Dijon mustard.

2. Using a hand whisk, slowly add the olive oil drop by drop, making sure that the oil is fully incorporated before adding more. Continue adding and whisking in the oil until you have a nice, thick mayo – you might not need to add all the oil.

3. Next, add the crushed garlic and the lemon zest and juice to the aïoli. Season generously with salt and pepper. Set aside in the fridge until needed.

4. To make the salt cod fritters, cut the salt cod into 5cm cubes.

5. Combine the flour and dried yeast in a mixing bowl. Make a well in the centre of the flour, then add the egg, 2 tablespoons of the honey and water to form a batter.

6. Pour enough oil for deep-frying into a deep-fryer or wide, deep pan, making sure it is no more than one-third full. Heat to 180°C, or until a cube of white bread browns in just under 1 minute.

7. Dip the salt cod cubes into the batter and then carefully lower them into the oil in batches and deep fry for 5 minutes, or until lightly golden. Remove the fritters from the oil with a slotted spoon and drain on paper towels.

8. Place a healthy dollop of the aïoli in the centre of a serving plate. Scatter some rocket leaves around the mound of aïoli then place the salt cod fritters on top of the leaves. Drizzle the plate with some extra honey.

Mixed Seafood with Saffron Sofrito

SERVES: **4**

200g bulgur wheat, cooked for 5 minutes,
then cooled
200g baby squid, cleaned
20 clams, rinsed
Grated zest and juice of 2 lemons

For the saffron sofrito
75ml olive oil
1 onion, finely diced
4 garlic cloves, finely sliced
150ml white wine
1 tablespoon chopped oregano
A pinch of saffron strands

To serve
Garlic mayo (see page 67)
Cucumber and tomato salad

Cooking 'en papillote' is a fancy term for baking in paper. The beauty of this method, which is perfect for fish and seafood, is that the flesh gently steams while all the aromatics are trapped inside the parcel. Also, less washing up.

1. Preheat the oven to 160°C fan/180°C/Gas 4. Cut eight pieces of baking parchment, each 35cm square.

2. To make the sofrito, heat the oil in a pan and gently fry the onion for 8 minutes, or until soft. Add the garlic and wine, then cook for a further 3 minutes. Add the oregano and saffron, then pour in 2 tablespoons of cold water, and cook for a further 8 minutes. Add the bulgur wheat to the pan, remove from the heat and set aside.

3. Slice the body of the squid into rings and the tentacles into large pieces.

4. Lay four squares of baking parchment on a flat surface. Next, lay four more squares over the first pieces, each at a slight angle to the first.

5. Spoon the bulgur wheat mixture onto the paper, then divide the squid and clams equally between all four. Add the lemon zest and juice.

6. Bring the edges of the baking parchment together and fold over to seal, wrapping up each to make an airtight parcel. Place on a roasting tray and cook in the hot oven for 12 minutes.

7. Place each seafood parcel on an individual plate. Tear open the seafood parcels, but discard any clams that have not opened. Serve with spoonfuls of garlic mayo and a fresh cucumber and tomato salad.

Prawns Pil Pil

SERVES: **4-6**

About 80ml olive oil
4 garlic cloves, sliced
1 teaspoon chilli flakes
450g king prawns, peeled and deveined,
tail shell left on
1 tablespoon dry sherry
Juice of 1 lemon
Chopped flat-leaf parsley
Generous pinch of smoked paprika

For the garlic mayonnaise
1 whole garlic bulb
200g mayonnaise
Juice of 1 lemon
15g chives, snipped

To serve
Sea salt
Lots of crusty bread

Prawns Pil Pil is a true classic Spanish tapas dish where succulent prawns are flash fried in a sizzling sauce of olive oil, garlic and chilli. So simple, but so tasty. Be aware that the residual heat in the pan will carry on cooking the prawns after you've taken them off the hob, so whip them off when they're almost cooked but not completely. There is nothing worse than a chewy, overcooked prawn.

1. Preheat the oven to 160°C fan/180°C/Gas 4. Place the whole garlic bulb on a small baking tray and roast in the oven for about 20 minutes, until soft. Remove and set aside to cool enough to handle, then squeeze the roasted garlic cloves from their skins and mix with the remaining mayonnaise ingredients.

2. Warm the oil in a frying pan with the sliced garlic and chilli flakes, then after 3 minutes turn up the heat, add the prawns and sauté for 5 minutes until pink and opaque. Add the sherry and lemon juice, then cook for a further 2 minutes.

3. Sprinkle the prawns with the chopped parsley and smoked paprika and serve sprinkled with sea salt, alongside plenty of crusty bread and the garlic mayo for dipping the prawns and bread into.

Images overleaf →

Cauliflower Cheese Tarts

MAKES: **4**

For the pastry
225g plain flour, plus extra for dusting
1 teaspoon salt
100g unsalted butter, diced, plus extra
for greasing
About 40ml ice-cold water

For the filling
½–1 head of cauliflower (depending on size),
broken into florets
100ml vegetable or sunflower oil
150g crème fraîche
3 medium eggs
200g strong red Cheddar, grated
100g Parmesan, finely grated
1 tablespoon Dijon mustard
Salt and black pepper

To serve
Tomato chutney

Cauliflower florets roasted to enhance their natural sweetness and then smothered in a two-cheese sauce makes the best cauliflower cheese. Pop that into perfectly crumbly pastry cases and job's a goodun.

1. To make the pastry, sift together the flour and salt. Using your fingertips, rub in the butter. Once it starts to resemble damp crumbs, add enough water to bring the mixture together. Press together to form a dough, wrap in clingfilm and chill in the fridge for 20 minutes.

2. Meanwhile, preheat the oven to 160°C fan/180°C/Gas 4 and grease four mini tart cases.

3. Divide the chilled pastry dough into four equal pieces. Roll out each piece into a circle on a lightly floured board. Line the mini tart cases with the rolled-out pastry, leaving the pastry overhanging the edges slightly.

4. Line the pastry cases with baking parchment and baking beans or dried pulses and blind bake for 20 minutes. Remove the baking beans and parchment and return to the oven for another 8–10 minutes, or until the pastry has dried out. Remove from the oven, but leave the oven on.

Continued overleaf →

If you're rubbing the butter into the flour with your fingers to make the pastry, work as quickly as you can to stop everything getting too warm and run your hands under cold water to keep them cool.

Alternatively, you can make the dough in a food processor to avoid handling it. Use the pulse setting and stop as soon as the mixture resembles breadcrumbs to prevent over-mixing, which makes the pastry tough.

Always chill the pastry dough before rolling it out. If you roll out the pastry before it's rested then it will shrink in the oven.

If you suffer from soggy bottoms, place a heavy baking sheet in the oven while it is heating up. When ready to cook, place the pastry-lined tart cases directly onto the heated tray.

5. Leave the pastry to cool completely on a wire cooling rack, then use a sharp knife to trim and neaten the edges.

6. Meanwhile, toss the cauliflower florets in the oil, season with salt and pepper, spread out on a baking tray and roast for 25 minutes, until just tender when pierced with a sharp knife, and nicely coloured on the surface.

7. Beat the crème fraîche with the eggs then stir in the two grated cheeses and the mustard.

8. Divide the roasted cauliflower florets between the part-baked pastry cases and spoon or pour over the egg mixture.

9. Bake for about 20 minutes, or until the filling is browned and bubbling, then leave the tarts to cool slightly before serving with tomato chutney.

Crispy Pea Arancini

These risotto balls filled with pea and pesto are absolute flavour bombs. Do give them a minute or two before serving as they'll be piping hot when straight from the deep fryer. As we say on the show, 'Don't burn your celebrity mouths.'

1. To make the pesto, blend all of the ingredients together until smooth. Set aside.

2. To make the arancini, melt the butter in a heavy-based pan. Add the rice and cook for 2–3 minutes over a low heat. When the rice starts to become a little translucent around the edges, add the wine and cook for another minute.

3. Add a ladleful of warm stock (it must be warm to enable the rice to cook properly). Once the rice has absorbed all the stock, add another ladleful. Repeat until all the stock has been used and/or the rice is tender.

4. Next, fold in the peas, spring onions and grated Parmesan and mascarpone and season well. Stir through a few spoonfuls of the pesto. Set aside until cool enough to handle, then roll the rice into small balls of about 30g each.

5. Roll the arancini in the flour, then the beaten egg, and finally in the breadcrumbs.

6. Pour enough oil for deep-frying into a deep-fryer or wide, deep pan, making sure it is no more than one-third full. Heat to 160°C, or until a cube of white bread browns in just over 1 minute. Carefully add batches of arancini and deep-fry for 4 minutes, until golden.

7. Serve the arancini with more of the pesto and some mustard mayo.

SERVES: **6**

For the arancini
50g butter
450g arborio rice
A splash of white wine
900ml warm vegetable stock
100g fresh or frozen peas, thawed
5 spring onions, finely chopped
150g Parmesan cheese, finely grated
50g mascarpone
75g plain flour
1 egg, beaten
200g brioche breadcrumbs
Vegetable oil, for deep-frying
Salt and black pepper

For the pesto
Large bunch of basil leaves
1 tablespoon pine nuts, roughly chopped
125g Pecorino cheese, finely grated
175ml extra virgin olive oil
1 garlic clove, roughly chopped

Moroccan Carrot
& Avocado Salad

SERVES: **6-8**

450g small carrots (or large ones cut into pieces about 120mm long)
150ml extra virgin olive oil
Grated zest and juice of 1 lemon and 1 orange
3 avocados
Grated zest and juice of 1 lime
25g watercress
3 Medjool dates, chopped
30g pumpkin seeds
15g dill, chopped
15g mint, chopped
125g radishes, sliced
Salt and black pepper

For the paste
3 garlic cloves
10g cumin seeds, toasted
1 teaspoon chilli flakes
1 teaspoon ground cinnamon
1 teaspoon ground coriander
2 tablespoons cider vinegar
1 teaspoon salt
Olive oil

For this warm salad, the carrots are roasted to enhance their natural sweetness, which is then amplified by the Medjool dates – a specialty of Morocco. The peppery radishes and nutty pumpkin seeds both provide a contrasting crunch to the creamy, smooth avocado flesh.

1. Preheat the oven to 160°C fan/180°C/Gas 4.

2. For the paste, blend the ingredients together with enough oil to form a paste.

3. Toss the carrots in the paste to coat, then spread out in a roasting tray and roast for 25 minutes.

4. Remove from the oven and spoon the carrots onto a serving platter. Whisk the extra virgin olive oil into the remnants of the cooking spices, together with the lemon and orange zest and juice. Spoon some of this dressing over the roasted carrots.

5. Scoop out the avocado flesh and gently crush with the lime zest and juice, seasoning well.

6. Put the watercress in a bowl with the dates, pumpkin seeds, dill and mint. Add the remaining dressing from the roasting tray and toss to coat.

7. Sit the salad on top of the carrots, then add the crushed avocado and sliced radishes to serve.

Cauliflower Fritters with Curry Mayo

SERVES: **4-6**

1 medium head of cauliflower, broken into florets
(450g florets)
50ml vegetable or sunflower oil
1 teaspoon cumin seeds
Vegetable oil, for deep-frying
Salt
Coriander leaves, to garnish

For the batter
1 medium egg
125ml ice-cold water
1 tablespoon sesame seeds
125g plain flour

For the curry mayo
125g mayonnaise
1 tablespoon curry paste
50ml sour cream

Cauliflower is truly a modern-day wonder ingredient. We must have cooked it in every way possible on the show – blanched, steamed, riced, raw, smothered in cheese sauce, subsituted for rice, even made into the base of a pizza. However, roasting the florets brings out its nutty sweetness and has to be one of the best ways to enjoy the humble cauli.

1. Preheat the oven to 180°C fan/200°C/Gas 6.

2. Toss the cauliflower florets in the oil and cumin seeds and spread out on a roasting tray. Sprinkle with salt and roast for 12–15 minutes.

3. For the curry mayo, mix the mayonnaise, curry paste and sour cream together.

4. For the batter, beat the egg and water together, then add the sesame seeds and a pinch of salt.

5. Put the flour in a bowl, make a well in the centre and pour in the beaten egg mixture.

6. Pour enough oil for deep-frying into a deep-fryer or wide, deep pan, making sure it is no more than one-third full. Heat to 180°C, or until a cube of white bread browns in just under 1 minute.

7. Dip the roasted cauliflower florets in the batter and deep-fry in batches in the hot oil for 3–4 minutes.

8. Serve the fritters sprinkled with coriander, and the curry mayo on the side.

Goat's Cheese Rarebit with Fig Jam

SERVES: **4-6**

50g unsalted butter
50g plain flour
175ml whole milk
300g hard goat's cheese, grated
1 tablespoon Dijon mustard
4–6 thick slices of walnut bread (or sourdough)

For the fig jam
300g figs, roughly chopped
1 tablespoon Pedro Ximénez sherry, or
1 teaspoon sherry vinegar
150g honey

Goat's cheese, walnuts and figs are some of the finest Middle Eastern ingredients and elevate this simple rarebit into something more than a little bit special.

1. For the jam, place the ingredients in a saucepan and bring to the boil. Reduce to a simmer and cook for 30 minutes, stirring occasionally, then allow to cool.

2. Melt the butter in a pan, add the flour and cook, stirring, for 2 minutes. Add the milk a little at a time, making sure it is smooth.

3. Take off the heat, whisk in the grated cheese and mustard and allow to cool a little. Preheat the grill to high.

4. Toast the bread and spread some of the jam on the toast.

5. Spoon the cheese mixture on top of the jam, then grill for 5–6 minutes until browned.

The spritz is the ultimate pre-dinner drink. A blend of sparkling prosecco and soda water can be mixed in endless ways, from tropical fruits to classic bitter liqueurs. Cheers!

Ian Burrell's Tropical Bling

SERVES: **1**

20ml coconut rum
20ml grapefruit soda
Champagne, to top up
Grapefruit peel, to garnish

1. Pour the coconut rum and grapefruit soda into a Champagne flute.

2. Top up the glass with Champagne and stir to mix.

3. Garnish with a twist of grapefruit peel.

Neil Ridley & Joel Harrison's Gin & Ginger Slushy

SERVES: **1**

30ml dry gin (such as Sipsmiths London Dry)
2 dashes of chocolate bitters (such as Bitter Truth or Mozart)
Ginger ale, to top up
A mint sprig, to garnish
A strip of lemon peel, to garnish
Icing sugar, to dust

1. Fill a white wine glass with finely crushed ice. Pour in the gin over the ice in the glass. Dash in the chocolate bitters. Top up the glass with ginger ale and add more ice.

2. Garnish with a sprig of mint, a thin strip of lemon peel and a light dusting of icing sugar.

Carl Brown's
Papaya Spritz

SERVES: **1**

For the papaya jelly
  (makes enough for 15–20 drinks)
500g papaya
250g sugar
100ml gin
70ml Campari
35ml vanilla extract

For the cocktail (per drink)
40ml papaya jelly
40ml soda water
70ml prosecco

1. To make the papaya jelly, place the papaya, sugar, gin, Campari and vanilla extract in a pan. Blend all the ingredients and gently warm until the sugar dissolves. Allow to cool and then chill in the fridge for 4 hours until the jelly has set. Chill until needed.

2. To make the cocktail, fill a large wine glass two thirds full with ice. Add the papaya jelly and soda water, then top up with prosecco. Stir with a spoon to mix.

Karina Elias's
Dreams

SERVES: **1**

For the pineapple vodka infusion
1 bottle vodka (such as Grey Goose)
½ fresh large pineapple, skin on but cut
  into chunks

For the tea infusion
3g jasmine pearl tea
3g white peony tea
3g rose tea

For the cocktail (per drink)
1 sugar cube
A few drops of orange blossom water
10ml pineapple vodka infusion (see above)
10ml tea infusions (see above)
Champagne, to top up

1. To make the pineapple vodka infusion, pour the vodka into a bowl and add the pineapple chunks. Leave to infuse overnight.

2. To make the three different tea infusions, pouring boiling water over the leaves. Leave each tea to steep for 10 minutes, but no longer otherwise the teas will turn bitter. Once brewed, combine the three teas,

3. Drop the sugar cube into a Champagne flute and add a few drops of orange blossom water onto the sugar.

4. Pour the pineapple vodka infusion and the tea infusions into the glass over the sugar cube and stir to combine. Top up the glass with Champagne.

quick & tasty

As each cookery segment on Sunday Brunch is only between 8 and 10 minutes long, we're well used to knocking out a tasty plate of food in record time. Sometimes it's a leisurely paced recipe that allows us plenty of time to chop and chat, while on other occasions things run over schedule – and that's when Simon goes into turbo cooking mode.

Whenever possible, we prefer to cook in real time on the show to demonstrate that it's completely possible to create a proper plate of food from start to finish in a matter of minutes. We do have a team of helpers onset to assist with the kitchen prep, which you won't have the luxury of at home, but even without these extra pairs of hands, every recipe in this chapter can be on the table within 30 minutes or less.

Rump Steak with Kale Salad

SERVES: **4**

4 x 300g dry-aged rump steaks (D-cut)
Oil
Salt and black pepper

For the dressing
8 anchovy fillets in oil (from a jar or can)
2 garlic cloves
50g capers
2 tablespoons Dijon mustard
1 teaspoon chilli flakes
1 teaspoon ground cumin
1 teaspoon smoked salt
1 teaspoon crushed black peppercorns
Grated zest and juice of 4 lemons
200ml extra virgin olive oil

For the salad
1 head of kale
1 red onion, very thinly sliced
30g pine nuts, toasted
30g sunflower seeds
150g Parmesan

One of our cooking mantras on the show is 'Oil the meat, not the pan.' That way, the steak will be covered evenly with the oil. There is only a few minutes leeway between a rare steak or one that is well done, so timing is crucial. Make sure the pan is really hot before adding the steak so you get that slightly sweet, charred outer crust.

1. Bring the steaks to room temperature. Heat a griddle pan until hot.

2. Rub the steaks with oil, season really well and char-grill in the pan for 3 minutes on each side. Remove from the pan and set aside to rest while you prepare the salad.

3. For the dressing, blend all the ingredients together until smooth.

4. For the salad, cut the stems out of the kale, then cut it into rough pieces. Put in a bowl, sprinkle over some salt and toss the kale for 2 minutes.

5. Now add the rest of the ingredients to the salad, except the Parmesan. Pour on the dressing, then toss gently.

6. Cut the rested steaks into slices about 1.5cm thick, and add to the dressed salad bowl. Grate over the Parmesan and serve.

Lamb Leg Steaks with Chimichurri & Sweet Potatoes

SERVES: **4**

450g sweet potatoes, roughly chopped
Vegetable oil, for cooking
4 lamb leg steaks
Salt and black pepper
Sesame seeds, to sprinkle

For the chimichurri
4 tablespoons red wine vinegar
1 teaspoon salt
1 garlic clove, finely chopped
1 shallot, finely diced
1 red chilli, finely chopped
40g rosemary leaves, chopped
25g parsley leaves, chopped
10g oregano leaves, chopped
100ml extra virgin olive oil

We've chargrilled these lamb leg steaks in a griddle pan but they would be equally delicious cooked over charcoal on a summer barbecue. Served with a simple chimichurri sauce packed with fresh herbs, this is summer on a plate.

1. Preheat the oven to 180°C fan/200°C/Gas 6.

2. Toss the sweet potato chunks in oil and plenty of seasoning. Spread out in a roasting tray or dish and roast for 25 minutes.

3. Meanwhile, to make the chimichurri, combine all the ingredients in a bowl and leave to stand for 20 minutes before serving.

4. Rub the lamb steaks with oil and season well. Preheat a ridged griddle pan until hot, then add the lamb and char-grill for 3 minutes on each side.

5. Serve the lamb steaks with the sweet potatoes and chimichurri, sprinkled with sesame seeds.

Pork Bun Cha

For the pork
500g minced pork
4 tablespoons Sriracha sauce
3 tablespoons fish sauce
Vegetable oil, for frying

For the nuoc mam cham sauce
125ml chicken or vegetable stock
3 tablespoons fish sauce
Juice of 2 limes
25g palm sugar, grated
2.5cm piece of fresh ginger, grated

For the noodles
200g cooked vermicelli noodles (100g uncooked)
50g beansprouts, washed
1 cucumber, julienned
1 carrot, julienned
½ daikon radish, julienned
1 spring onion, sliced
Handful each of Thai basil, coriander and mint
1 bird's-eye chilli, finely chopped

Singer and actor Will Young was one of our guests the Sunday we made this delicious, Vietnamese-inspired pork noodle bowl. Will is always a welcome visitor – he's so tidy that he keeps his work station neat and gives our studio kitchen a thorough clean.

1. For the pork, mix the pork mince and sauces together, mould into about 16 balls, then flatten each ball into a patty shape.

2. Working in batches, heat a little oil in a frying pan, add the pork patties and fry for 3 minutes on each side, until browned and cooked through. Set aside to keep warm.

3. For the sauce, put all the ingredients into a pan and heat until the sugar has dissolved, then remove and leave to cool slightly.

4. For the noodles, combine all the ingredients and divide between four bowls. Add the sauce and top with the pork patties.

Pork Loin with Salted Caramel Potatoes

SERVES: **4**

For the pork
350g pork tenderloin
50g unsalted butter
100ml dry cider
1 tablespoon cider vinegar
3 tablespoons redcurrant jelly
Salt and black pepper

For the seed crust
1 tablespoon fennel seeds
1 tablespoon coarse sea salt
2 teaspoons cracked black peppercorns

For the salted caramel potatoes
125g sugar
50ml cold water
450g new or fingerling potatoes, boiled and cooled
120g unsalted butter
1 tablespoon smoked sea salt

The fragrant fennel seed crust on the tenderloin provides a punchy contrast to the sweet pork meat. When making the caramel for the potatoes, do not be tempted to stir or shake the pan until all the sugar has dissolved and turned golden.

1. Preheat the oven to 160°C fan/180°C/Gas 4.

2. For the seed crust, place the fennel seeds, sea salt and black peppercorns in a pestle and mortar and crush until broken down but still coarse.

3. Rub the crushed seeds all over the pork.

4. Place a frying pan over a high heat and fry the pork for 6 minutes to seal the meat, turning it until all sides are golden and the seeds form a crust.

5. Transfer the pork to a roasting tin and roast for 12–15 minutes, then remove from the oven and add the butter to the tin. Baste the pork with the melted butter and transfer to a plate. Set aside in a warm place. Do not wipe out the tin.

6. Add the cider, vinegar and redcurrant jelly to the roasting tin. Bring to the boil to reduce to a sauce, season and set aside to keep warm.

7. For the potatoes, heat the sugar and water in a pan over a low heat until the sugar has dissolved. Increase the heat and cook, without stirring, until it starts to bubble and turn golden, then take off the heat (it will carry on cooking).

8. Add the potatoes and butter to the caramel, mix well and simmer for 10 minutes until coated and sticky. Add the smoked sea salt.

9. Slice the pork into thick slices and serve with the potatoes and reduced juices.

Spiced Chicken with Green Rice

This mildly spiced chicken is enlivened by the zing of lime juice and the punch of fresh chillies, both common ingredients in Mexican cooking. Green rice – or arroz verde – is a popular Mexican side dish and is a brilliant way to cook rice that packs it full of flavour and gives it a vibrant colour.

1. Preheat the oven to 180°C fan/200°C/Gas 6.

2. Toss the chicken strips in the oil, honey, oregano, garlic, lime zest and juice, chillies and salt, spread out on a sheet of baking parchment in a roasting tray and bake for about 12–15 minutes, or until cooked through.

3. To make the rice, heat the oil in a pan, add the spring onions and garlic and gently fry for 5 minutes.

4. Add the rice and stir well, then add the stock, bring to the boil, cover and simmer for 15 minutes. Take off the heat, stir in the butter and peas and leave to stand for 5 minutes.

5. In a processor, blend the spinach, coriander and vinegar together, then stir into the rice.

6. Serve the rice in a big bowl, topped with the chicken strips and more coriander leaves sprinkled over.

SERVES: **4**

4 chicken breasts, each cut into 4 long strips
1 tablespoon olive oil
3 tablespoons runny honey
15g fresh oregano, chopped
1 garlic clove, crushed
Grated zest and juice of 1 lime
2 green chillies, finely chopped
1 teaspoon salt

For the rice
1 tablespoon vegetable oil
4 spring onions, chopped
1 garlic clove, chopped
200g jasmine rice
450ml chicken stock
50g unsalted butter
50g peas
70g spinach
Bunch of coriander, plus extra to serve
3 tablespoons white wine vinegar

Ultimate Fish Finger Butty

For the fish fingers
500g haddock, skin removed
25g fine sea salt
100g panko breadcrumbs
100g fresh breadcrumbs
100g plain flour
2 eggs, beaten
Vegetable oil, for shallow-frying
50g butter

For the tartare sauce
150g mayonnaise
50g salad cream
30g capers, chopped
50g gherkins, chopped
Salt and black pepper

To serve
8 slices of thick-cut white bread (we prefer
Warburton's Toastie), buttered
3 tablespoons Sriracha sauce
Skin-on fat chips
Ketchup, for dipping

When selecting the haddock to make these fish fingers, don't buy the thin tail piece. Go for the loin because it is nice and thick. That way, you'll be able to cut the fish into good, chunky, fat fingers. Of course, the choice of sauce for a butty comes down to personal preference, but we urge you to try this combo of homemade tartare alongside a squeeze of Sriracha.

1. To make the tartare sauce, mix the mayonnaise, salad cream, capers and gherkins together. Season to taste.

2. Cut the fish into chunky fingers the exact width of the slices of bread. You need 3 fingers per butty, or 4 if you prefer skinny fingers (but we like 'em fat). Sprinkle the salt over the fish and leave for 20 minutes, then immerse the fingers in a bowl of cold water to rinse, remove and pat dry with kitchen paper.

3. Pulse the panko and fresh breadcrumbs together until smooth and fine.

4. Put the flour, eggs and breadcrumbs into 3 separate shallow bowls. Dip the fish pieces in the flour, then in the egg, then in the crumbs, to coat.

Continued overleaf →

Salting the fish draws out the moisture from the flesh prior to cooking, so the fish fingers remain firm and don't lose their shape or shrink. You can use a 50/50 mix of salt and sugar, which imparts a delicious sweetness to the fish.

5. Heat about a 1.5cm depth of oil in a frying pan. Shallow-fry the fish fingers for 3 minutes on each side, or until golden on the crumb. Flip over and repeat, adding the butter at the end of the cooking for richness. Drain on kitchen paper.

6. To serve, add a smear of tartare sauce to half the slices of buttered bread. Place the fish fingers – 3 per slice – on top. Drizzle over the Sriracha sauce, then press another slice of bread on top of the fish fingers and then cut the sandwiches in half.

7. Serve with fat chips, and feel free to dip the butties into ketchup too.

Tim's Kung Fu Tuna

SERVES: **2**

2 x 250g tuna loin steaks
Vegetable oil, for oiling, cooking and deep-frying
200g broad, flat rice noodles

For the marinade
2 garlic cloves, finely chopped
1 thumb-sized piece of fresh ginger, grated
2 tablespoons vegetable oil
100ml light soy sauce
2 tablespoons fish sauce
2 tablespoons rice vinegar
Juice of 1 lime
2 tablespoons runny honey

For the vegetables
1 fennel bulb, cut into strips
½ cucumber, cut into strips
1 large carrot, cut into batons
3 spring onions, sliced into lengths
1 red pepper, cut into strips
1 tablespoon sesame seeds

To serve
1 chilli, sliced
2 spring onions, sliced

Tim dreamt up this quick-cook tuna dish to showcase his newly acquired chopping skills. He'd recently taught himself how to chop vegetables into long, thin matchsticks (or julienne) and, well, he wanted to show off a bit. Despite the best efforts of guest host Johnny Vegas to distract Tim from his cooking, this dish made it on to the plate and was an instant hit with viewers. It even inspired one watcher to create a signature song, 'Be the Tuna'.

1. Mix together all the marinade ingredients then add the tuna, turn to coat and leave to marinate for 1–2 hours.

2. Heat a frying pan until very hot. Remove the tuna from the marinade and lightly oil using 1 teaspoon oil. Seal the steaks for 1–2 minutes on each side in the pan, then remove and set aside to rest.

3. Heat 1 tablespoon of oil in the frying pan and stir-fry all the vegetables for 2–3 minutes. Pour a few tablespoons of the marinade over to coat, then add the sesame seeds.

4. Pour enough oil for deep-frying into a deep-fryer or wide, deep pan, making sure it is no more than one-third full. Heat to 180°C, or until a cube of white bread browns in just under 1 minute.

5. Deep-fry the rice noodles until puffed, then remove to a tray lined with kitchen paper.

6. Serve the tuna on top of the veg, sprinkled with the chilli and spring onions, and with the deep-fried noodles on the side.

Sweet & Sour
Crispy Fish Bites

SERVES: **4**

500g cod, cut into 40mm pieces
Vegetable oil, for deep-frying

For the sauce
2 tablespoons vegetable oil
½ red onion, cut into 1.5–2cm pieces
1 red and 1 green pepper, cut the same way as the onion
2.5cm piece of fresh ginger, cut into matchsticks
3 tablespoons tomato ketchup
50g pineapple chunks from a tin
175ml pineapple juice from the tin of chunks
2 tablespoons white wine vinegar
2 tablespoons sugar
1 tablespoon cornflour, mixed with a little water to form a paste

For the batter
110g plain flour
Pinch of baking powder
1 tablespoon cornflour
1 teaspoon salt
Pinch of ground turmeric
175ml ice-cold sparkling water

Battered fish doesn't always have to be served up with chips. For an Asian flavour, team these crispy cod bites with tangy sweet and sour sauce. Served with steamed basmati rice, this dish can be on the table quicker than your local takeaway can deliver.

1. To make the sauce, heat the oil in a pan, add the onion, peppers and ginger and fry for 2–3 minutes.

2. Add the ketchup and cook for 1 minute, then add everything else except the cornflour paste. Bring to the boil, simmer for 5 minutes, then add the cornflour and cook for 2 minutes more.

3. Mix the dry ingredients for the batter in a bowl, add the sparkling water and whisk it all together. Leave to stand for 20 minutes.

4. Pour enough oil for deep-frying into a deep-fryer or wide, deep pan, making sure it is no more than one-third full. Heat to 180°C, or until a cube of white bread browns in just under 1 minute.

5. Dip the fish pieces into the batter and deep-fry in batches for 5 minutes, then drain and serve with a bowl of sauce to dip in.

Charred Salmon
Santa Fe Caesar

SERVES: **4**

4 x 150g salmon fillets
Oil, for rubbing
2 gem lettuce heads, quartered lengthways
About 36 croûtons (shop-bought is fine)
1 red onion, finely sliced
12 salted anchovy fillets
Salt and black pepper

For the dressing
250g mayonnaise
2 tablespoons Dijon mustard
2 tablespoons white wine vinegar
1 garlic clove
100g Parmesan, grated
1 teaspoon cayenne pepper

To serve
Lime wedges
Pickled chillies

Whoever came up with the idea of cooking lettuce is, frankly, a genius. While it might seem strange at first, trust us, charring a wedge of gem lettuce gives it a delicate sweetness. The charred lettuce and blackened salmon brings a new spin on the classic Caesar salad.

1. Preheat the oven to 200°C fan/220°C/Gas 7.

2. For the dressing, blend everything together, adding a drop of water if it seems too thick. (This makes more dressing than you will need; the rest can be stored in the fridge.)

3. Heat a griddle or frying pan until hot. Rub the salmon fillets with oil and season them, then cook in the pan for 2 minutes on each side. Transfer to a baking tray and finish cooking in the oven for 4 minutes, then remove and set aside.

4. Add the gem lettuce quarters to the pan and cook for 15–20 seconds on each cut side, to char. Remove to a serving plate or dish.

5. Pile the lettuce up with croutons, sliced red onion and anchovies, and finish with some dressing.

6. Sit the salmon alongside, with lime wedges and pickled chillies.

Firecracker Salmon

SERVES: **4**

300g honey
200ml Cholula hot sauce
2 red chillies, sliced
120g unsalted butter
75ml balsamic vinegar
75ml light soy sauce
4 x 175g salmon fillets

For the salad
400g cooked giant couscous (200g uncooked)
8 spring onions, chopped
12 fine green beans, blanched and cut into
short lengths
100g cashews, toasted and roughly chopped
100g spinach, finely shredded

To serve
Handful each of coriander and mint leaves,
chopped
Lime wedges

The Cholula hot sauce in the glaze used on the fish brings the fiery flavour that lends this salmon dish its name. Sweet, tangy and spicy, this sauce has everything.

1. Preheat the oven to 180°C fan/200°C/Gas 6.

2. Put the honey, hot sauce, chillies, butter, vinegar and soy in a pan and heat until combined.

3. Lay the salmon in a dish, pour over about two-thirds of the sauce and bake for 12 minutes.

4. Meanwhile, mix the salad ingredients together, pour over the remaining sauce and mix well.

5. Flake the salmon into the mix and add all the sauce from the dish.

6. Serve with the herbs and lime.

Freekeh & Edamame Salad with Tamarind Yoghurt Dressing

SERVES: **4**

250g cooked freekeh (125g uncooked)
6 spring onions, finely chopped
125g edamame beans (frozen are fine)
125g salted cashews
Handful of baby salad leaves
1 tablespoon chopped mint, plus extra leaves
to serve
1 wholemeal pitta, toasted and torn into croûtons
4 ripe tomatoes, chopped
Grated zest of 1 lemon

For the dressing
150g yoghurt
Grated zest and juice of 1 lemon
2 tablespoons honey
2 tablespoons tamarind sauce/paste
2.5cm piece of fresh ginger, grated
1 garlic clove, grated
Salt and black pepper

This simple spring salad combines freekeh (a nutty, slightly chewy grain) with bouncy edamame beans, ripe tomatoes and dry, crisp croûtons – it's a real rollercoaster of textures. Tamarind is a useful storecupboard ingredient that adds a subtle tang to sauces and dressings. Because it tastes similar to dates, although with a less sweet, slightly sour note, tamarind is sometimes called the Indian date. You may have unknowingly tasted it before if you've ever used that condiment classic Worcester sauce.

1. For the dressing, simply mix all the ingredients together well with seasoning to taste.

2. Put the freekeh, spring onions, edamame beans, cashews, baby leaves and chopped mint into a bowl.

3. Add the dressing and mix it through, then tip into a serving bowl.

4. Top the salad with the pitta croûtons, chopped tomatoes, lemon zest and extra mint leaves, then serve.

Aubergine Schnitzel with Salsa Verde

SERVES: **4-6**

100g plain flour
100g breadcrumbs
100g vegetarian Parmesan-style cheese, finely grated
Grated zest of 1 lemon
2 eggs, beaten
2 aubergines, cut lengthways into 1–1.5cm-thick slices
5–6 tablespoons sunflower oil
50g butter
Salt and black pepper

For the salsa verde
Bunch of flat-leaf parsley, finely chopped
Bunch of mint, finely chopped
½ bunch of tarragon, finely chopped
1 tablespoon capers, finely chopped
1 tablespoon Dijon mustard
125ml olive oil

To serve
Lemon halves, to squeeze

These aubergine schnitzels are up there in our all-time top veggie-friendly dishes. The creamy soft flesh of the aubergine almost melts away in contrast to the crunchy crumb coating. Of course, you can use regular Parmesan if you're cooking for non-vegetarians. Sometimes we serve this with a few tomatoes that have been roughly chopped, warmed in the pan and then drizzled with good olive oil.

1. To make the salsa verde, mix all the ingredients together well in a bowl.

2. Add a generous pinch each of salt and pepper to the flour and put in a shallow bowl. Mix the breadcrumbs with the grated cheese and lemon zest and put in a separate shallow bowl. Put the beaten eggs in a third shallow bowl.

3. Dip the aubergine slices first in the seasoned flour, then the egg, then the breadcrumb mixture, to coat on both sides.

4. Heat the oil and butter together in a frying pan (how much oil you need will depend on the size of your pan) until hot, then add the coated aubergine slices and fry for 3 minutes on each side until cooked through and golden on the outside.

5. Serve the aubergine schnitzels with the salsa verde and lemon halves to squeeze over, and maybe some chopped tomatoes in olive oil.

Cauliflower Biryani Salad

1 tablespoon ground turmeric
1 head of cauliflower, cut or broken into
large florets
3 tablespoons white wine vinegar
5 tablespoons extra virgin olive oil

For the curry paste
1 onion, roughly chopped
5cm piece of fresh ginger, roughly chopped
3 garlic cloves, roughly chopped
1 tablespoon curry powder
2 teaspoons ground cumin
3 tablespoons vegetable oil
2 red chillies, chopped

For the quinoa salad
400g cooked quinoa (from a packet, or from
200g uncooked)
100g frozen peas, defrosted
100g fine green beans (kept raw), halved
50g cashews, toasted
Handful of chopped coriander

For the carrot garnish
4 carrots, cut into fine matchsticks
1 teaspoon granulated sugar
Grated zest and juice of 1 lemon
3cm piece of fresh ginger, grated
1 teaspoon cumin seeds, toasted

Another outing for the wonder-ingredient that is cauliflower, this time in a lightly spiced salad that is chock full of crunch. While it can be made ahead and stored in the fridge, this salad is best served at room temperature, so fridge it before adding the dressing to it. When ready to serve, bring the salad back up to room temperature and then add the dressing.

1. Preheat the oven to 180°C fan/200°C/Gas 6.

2. For the carrot garnish, combine all the ingredients and leave for at least 20 minutes.

3. Meanwhile, bring a pan of water to the boil and add the turmeric. Blanch the cauliflower florets in the turmeric water for 1 minute, then refresh in cold water and drain.

4. Blitz all the ingredients for the curry paste in food processor, blending until smooth.

5. Gently fry the curry paste in a frying pan for 4 minutes, then cool.

6. Take one third of the curry paste and rub it over the cauliflower florets. Spread out on a roasting tray and roast for 6 minutes.

7. Blend the rest of the curry paste with the vinegar and oil, to make a dressing.

8. Mix the salad ingredients together and fold in the dressing.

9. Serve the quinoa salad topped with the roasted cauliflower florets and carrot garnish.

Mushroom Puri

SERVES: **4-6**

For the mushroom curry
4 tablespoons vegetable oil
450g chestnut mushrooms, sliced
1 red onion, finely chopped
2 garlic cloves, crushed
2.5cm piece of fresh ginger, grated
1 green bird's-eye chilli, finely chopped
1 tablespoon medium curry paste
2 tablespoons malt vinegar
5 tablespoons double cream

For the puri
250g chapati flour
About 125ml warm water
1 tablespoon chopped coriander
1 teaspoon salt
Vegetable oil, for deep-frying

To garnish
1 small green chilli, finely chopped
Handful of coriander leaves

Mushrooms are a fantastic ingredient and bring so much flavour to a dish. We cook mushrooms pretty often on the show and have learnt that the best way to cook them is to pop them in the pan and then step away – the mushrooms will tell you when they are ready as they'll speak to you, you just need to listen out for the squeak…

1. To make the puri, mix the flour, water, coriander and salt together in a bowl, cover and chill in the fridge for 20 minutes.

2. Meanwhile, to make the mushroom curry, heat 3 tablespoons of the oil in a frying pan and add the mushrooms. Fry for 5 minutes, but don't shake the pan; let them caramelise. Remove from the pan and set aside.

3. Add the remaining tablespoon of oil to the pan and gently fry the onion, garlic, ginger and chilli for 5 minutes, or until soft. Add the curry paste and cook for 4 minutes. Add the vinegar, stir, then return the mushrooms to the pan. Set aside.

4. Divide the puri dough into 6 pieces and roll out each piece into a 15cm disc (cut them if you want a perfect round).

5. Pour enough oil for deep-frying into a deep-fryer or wide, deep pan, making sure it is no more than one-third full. Heat to 180°C, or until a cube of white bread browns in just under 1 minute.

6. Add the puri one at a time and deep-fry for about 45 seconds, turning once.

7. Reheat the curry if necessary, and stir through the cream. Serve the puri with curry on top, garnished with the chopped chilli and coriander.

Chilli Aubergines with Smoked Feta

SERVES: **4**

2 aubergines, cut into decent-sized chunks
Vegetable oil, for frying
125g smoked (you can use plain) feta, crumbled
1 tablespoon sesame seeds
2 spring onions, finely chopped
1 red chilli, finely sliced

For the sauce
2 tablespoons brown sugar
3 tablespoons rice vinegar
3 tablespoons light soy sauce
50g chilli paste
Grated zest and juice of 1 lime

Gooey, sticky, squidgy, these chilli aubergines make a phenomenal quick supper. The smooth, cooling feta accentuates the creaminess of the aubergine flesh but also contrasts the heat of the chilli. You can serve these aubergines alongside some mini rice crackers. Either way, it's 100% delicious.

1. Put all the sauce ingredients into a saucepan and boil for 5 minutes, then remove the pan from the heat.

2. Fry the aubergines in oil in a frying pan for 5–6 minutes, turning, until cooked and soft.

3. Add the sauce to the frying pan and cook for 2–3 minutes, until sticky.

4. Serve the aubergines in a bowl topped with the feta, sesame seeds, spring onions and chilli.

Cocktails don't have to be complicated.
These delicious drinks are all made by simply sloshing
just a few ingredients in a jug, glass or shaker. Cheers!

Ian Burrell's
Reggae Rum Punch

SERVES: **4**

200ml over-proofed rum (such as
    Wray & Nephew)
250ml pineapple juice
250ml orange juice
100ml fresh lime juice
100ml grenadine syrup
Slices of orange, to garnish
Slices of pineapple, to garnish
Slices of lime, to garnish

1. Fill a pitcher or jug with plenty of ice. Pour in the rum, pineapple juice, orange juice, lime juice and grenadine syrup into the pitcher over the ice.

2. Add slices of orange, pineapples and lime to the pitcher.

Karina Elias's
Bourbon Mule

SERVES: **1**

50ml bourbon (such as Four Roses)
15ml freshly squeezed lime juice
15ml sugar syrup
Ginger beer, to top up
Piece of crystallised ginger, to garnish

1. Pour the bourbon into tall Collins glass. Add the lime juice and sugar syrup.

2. Top up the glass with ginger beer and stir until well mixed. Add some ice cubes.

3. Garnish the drink with a piece of crystallised ginger.

Neil Ridley & Joel Harrison's
The Ocho Paloma

SERVES: **1**

50ml tequila (such as Ocho Tequila)
30ml freshly squeezed pink grapefruit juice
15ml freshly squeezed lime juice
15ml agave syrup
Pink grapefruit or pompelmo soda, to top up
Pink grapefruit wedge, to garnish

1. Add all ingredients to a shaker and shake with cubed ice. Shake the first ingredients over ice

2. Fill a tall glass with ice cubes, then strain the contents of the shaker into the glass.

3. Top up the glass with the grapefruit or pompelmo soda.

4. Garnish with a pink grapefruit wedge.

Carl Brown's
Indian Punch

SERVES: **1**

300ml genever gin
60ml maraschino liqueur
300ml water
100ml freshly squeezed lemon juice
50g sugar

1. Rub the sugar into the rind of the lemons and add to a pitcher or jug. Add the lemon juice to the pitcher and stir until the sugar has dissolved.

2. Add the gin, maraschino liqueur and water to the pitcher and stir to mix.

3. Add ice to the pitcher to chill.

4. Serve the punch over more ice.

forged

Slow-cooked dishes are possibly our most favourite kinds of meals to cook and eat. Once you've cracked through a bit of prep work up front, you're then free to spend a few hours (hey, why not spend that time watching Sunday Brunch?!) whilst the heat of the oven works its magic on the ingredients as they meld together in the pot.

Tim says slow-cooked meals are like the best kind of Christmas present. You make a list, do the shopping, wrap it all up in a pot and then forgedaboudit until its time to sit down with the fam and tuck in. Opened up at the table, a slow-cooked dish will release its aromas in puffs of steam and everyone will collapse into admiring oohs and aahs. Guaranteed.

Mutton Mussaman Curry

225g potatoes, peeled and diced
2 teaspoons ground turmeric
2 tablespoons vegetable oil
600g mutton, cut into big chunks (7–8cm cubes)
250ml coconut cream
1 x 400ml tin of coconut milk
Splash of fish sauce
4 tablespoons tamarind paste
1 cinnamon stick
1 tablespoon palm sugar

For the paste
6 chillies
3 shallots, peeled
5 garlic cloves, peeled
2 lemongrass stalks
2.5cm piece of fresh ginger
1 teaspoon cumin seeds
1 tablespoon coriander seeds
2 cloves
6 black peppercorns
1 teaspoon shrimp paste
1 teaspoon sugar
2 tablespoons vegetable oil

To serve
Jasmine rice
50g roasted peanuts, roughly chopped

The mutton will release quite a bit of oil, which you can skim off the surface. If you have time, make this the day before and chill it, then the fat will solidify and be easier to remove. You can use lamb in place of mutton; we source ours from a specialist butcher in the Lake District, and the meat has a great depth of flavour.

1. To make the paste, dry-fry the chillies, shallots, garlic, lemongrass, ginger, cumin and coriander seeds, cloves and peppercorns for 5–6 minutes.

2. Transfer the paste to a food processor with the shrimp paste, sugar and vegetable oil and blend until smooth.

3. Boil the potatoes with the turmeric added to the water (this gives them a lovely colour) until tender, then drain and leave to cool.

4. Meanwhile, heat the oil in a heavy-based pan or flameproof casserole, add the diced mutton and seal all over, then remove to a bowl.

5. Add the paste to the pan and cook for a few minutes until it becomes fragrant.

6. Stir in the coconut cream a little at a time, then add the coconut milk and bring to the boil. Add the fish sauce, tamarind, cinnamon and sugar. Return the mutton to the pan, cover and cook over a gentle heat for 1 hour 30 minutes.

7. Add the potatoes to the curry, warm through and serve with jasmine rice, with the peanuts sprinkled over.

Korean Sticky Pork Belly

SERVES: **6-8**

1kg pork belly, cut into slices
100ml light soy sauce
100g red Korean chilli paste
3 tablespoons rice vinegar
3 tablespoons honey
1 tablespoon sesame oil
4 garlic cloves, grated
3cm piece of fresh ginger, grated

To serve
2 spring onions, finely sliced on the diagonal
1 teaspoon sesame seeds
1 cucumber, halved, deseeded and shredded
Steamed rice

This slow-cooked sticky pork belly is crunchy on the outside but falling-apart tender on the inside. Cutting the pork belly into slices before roasting maximises the surface area for added crunch. The heat of the oven pretty much does all the heavy lifting here – you're only required to do a little light chopping.

1. Preheat the oven to 180°C fan/200°C/Gas 6.

2. Pat the pork dry with kitchen paper.

3. Mix the remaining ingredients together to make a sauce.

4. Toss the pork slices in the sauce and transfer everything to a roasting dish. Cover the dish with foil and roast in the oven for 1 hour 30 minutes.

5. Preheat the grill to high.

6. Take off the foil then remove the meat and grill for 3 minutes on each side (feel free to brush a little sauce on).

7. Serve the pork with sliced spring onions and sesame seeds sprinkled over, with steamed rice and shredded cucumber on the side.

Sausage & Chorizo Goulash

This Spanish-style one-pot winter warmer gets an extra kick of paprika from the chorizo, which packs so much flavour into a dish. Chorizo is a favourite ingredient for both of us and we use it often when cooking at home and in the studio. One time, when we were cooking with comedian James Acaster, Simon splashed a little sherry onto his frying chorizo and…Whoosh! Flames shot right up into the lighting rig suspended above the studio kitchen. But it was okay. We carried on as if nothing had happened and we're pretty sure no-one noticed.

SERVES: **4-6**

1 tablespoon olive oil
900g good-quality beef sausages, each cut into 4 pieces
300g spicy cooking chorizo, sliced into coins
2 onions, finely sliced
1 garlic clove, chopped
1 red pepper, very finely sliced
2 red chillies, finely chopped
1 tablespoon smoked paprika
200ml beef stock
2 x 400g tins of butter beans, rinsed and drained

To serve
175ml sour cream
1 tablespoon chopped parsley
Steamed rice or mashed potato

1. Preheat the oven to 130°C fan/150°C/Gas 2.

2. Heat the oil in an ovenproof pan or flameproof dish that has a lid, add the sausage pieces and chorizo and fry until crisp.

3. Remove the sausage and chorizo from the pan and set aside, then add the onions and garlic to the same pan.

4. Add the pepper, chillies and smoked paprika, then return the fried sausage and chorizo to the pan and add the stock.

5. Cover with a lid, transfer to the oven and cook for 30 minutes, then remove from the oven and skim off any fat from the surface.

6. Add the butter beans and cook for a further 10 minutes in the oven. When ready to serve, stir through the sour cream and parsley, and serve with rice or mashed potato.

Lamb Shawarma

SERVES: **8-10**

3 onions, sliced
6 garlic cloves, sliced
150ml red wine vinegar
150ml chicken stock
2.5kg lamb shoulder, butterflied (you can ask your butcher to do this for you)
100g harissa paste or ras el hanout paste
1 tablespoon smoked paprika
1 tablespoon ground cinnamon
1 tablespoon sumac
2 tablespoons sea salt
3 tablespoons port

For the cucumber salad
2 cucumbers, peeled, halved, deseeded and cut into thick half-moons
2 teaspoons chilli flakes
1 tablespoon sea salt
Grated zest and juice of 1 lemon

For the sauce
100ml Greek yoghurt
100ml tahini
½ roasted garlic bulb (see page 67)

To serve
Turkish flatbreads (or naan)
Chopped tomatoes
Pickled chillies
Shredded lettuce
Sumac, to sprinkle

Slowly steamed on a bed of onions, this lamb becomes so meltingly tender you can easily pull it into shreds. For the rub, use ras el hanout for a warm, aromatic note, or if you prefer more heat, opt for fiery harissa.

1. Preheat the oven to 140°C fan/160°C/Gas 3.

2. Put the sliced onions and garlic in a roasting tin and pour over the vinegar and stock.

3. Trim most of the fat off the lamb and sit it on top of the onions and garlic. Rub the harissa or ras el hanout paste over the lamb. Combine the smoked paprika, cinnamon, sumac and salt and sprinkle evenly over the harissa-covered lamb. Pour the port around the sides of the lamb.

4. Cover tightly with a layer of baking parchment then one of foil, to make a double layer. Roast for 4 hours, then remove the parchment and foil and roast for a further 1 hour to crisp up, adding a little water to the base if it's drying out. Shred the meat using 2 forks.

5. Meanwhile, mix the cucumber half-moons with the chilli flakes and salt. Leave to stand for 1 hour before adding the lemon zest and juice.

6. To make the sauce, mix together the yoghurt, tahini and roasted garlic, squeezing the insides of the garlic from the skins.

7. Place a mound of meat with all the trimmings on a flatbread, drizzle over some sauce (thin it with a little water if it seems too thick) and sprinkle with sumac to serve.

Images overleaf →

Pork Ribs with
Honey Mustard Slaw

SERVES: **4–6**

1kg baby back pork ribs, cut into 5–6-bone pieces
Lemon wedges, to serve

For the marinade
4 onions, roughly chopped
6 garlic cloves, roughly chopped
1 tablespoon each of rosemary, marjoram and
oregano
1 tablespoon tomato purée
125ml white wine
5 tablespoons tomato ketchup
2 tablespoons brown sauce
2 tablespoons light soy sauce
30g beef stock powder, with enough water added
to make a paste

For the slaw
3 tablespoons honey
3 tablespoons wholegrain mustard
5 tablespoons mayonnaise
½ head of celeriac
½ fennel bulb, finely sliced
6 spring onions, sliced
Handful of parsley, finely chopped

These sweet baby back pork ribs are marinated for several hours so all the flavours can permeate the meat, but they are then quick to cook in the oven. The crunchy slaw is the perfect accompaniment. The celeriac might not be much to look at before it's cut into matchsticks, but its subtle celery taste pairs beautifully with the strong aniseed flavour of fennel.

1. Cook the pork ribs for 45 minutes in simmering water, then drain and place in a wide, shallow dish.

2. Put all the marinade ingredients into a food processor and purée to a paste. Set aside about a quarter.

3. Pour the rest of the marinade over the ribs and leave for at least 4 hours, but ideally overnight, in the fridge.

4. Preheat the oven to 140°C fan/160°C/Gas 3. Spread the ribs out in a roasting tin and cook for about 20 minutes.

5. Meanwhile, for the slaw, mix the honey, mustard and mayonnaise together in a bowl. Using a mandoline, grate the celeriac. If you don't have a mandoline, slice the celeriac extremely finely and then cut into matchsticks. Add all the remaining slaw ingredients to the honey mustard mayo and mix.

6. Heat the reserved marinade mixture in a pan, brush it onto the ribs and serve with the slaw and lemon wedges, and some bread.

Porchetta Spiced Pork

SERVES: 6-8

2.5kg pork shoulder, butterflied (you can ask your butcher to do this for you)
2 onions, sliced
3 bay leaves
5 tablespoons red wine vinegar
5 tablespoons Marsala

For the rub
1 tablespoon each of black peppercorns, fennel seeds, coriander seeds and chilli flakes
15g rosemary leaves, chopped
1 tablespoon coarse sea salt
5 garlic cloves
Grated zest of 1 orange

For the potatoes
100g butter
300g new potatoes, cooked and halved unless small
100g spinach
20g oregano leaves, chopped
Grated zest and juice of 1 lemon

Porchetta is the classic Italian dish of pork rolled with garlic and herbs, then slow roasted to crisp cracking perfection. Here, we've gone the other way – rather than roll up the pork into a tight bundle, we've butterflied the pork to flatten it out. Wrapped in foil and cooked over a bed of onions, the melting meat will shred easily once cooked.

1. Preheat the oven to 140°C fan/160°C/Gas 3.

2. To make the rub, grind all the ingredients together in a spice blender.

3. Remove most of the outside fat of the pork. Put the sliced onions in the base of a roasting tin, add the bay leaves and pour over the vinegar and Marsala.

4. Sit the pork on top and apply the rub all over the pork, using your hands.

5. Cover the tin with foil and cook for 3 hours and 30 minutes, then remove the foil and cook for a further 1 hour.

6. Shred or slice the pork and let it sit in the juices in the tin.

7. Meanwhile, melt the butter in a large frying pan until foaming, add the potatoes and let them brown a little, then toss and repeat. Add the spinach, oregano and lemon zest and juice to the pan and cook for 5 minutes.

8. Serve the pork and potatoes with crusty Italian bread.

Veal Shoulder with Gorgonzola Polenta

SERVES: **6**

1 tablespoon vegetable oil
2 onions, very finely sliced
2 carrots, finely sliced
750g veal shoulder, cut into large chunks (about 5cm)
1 tablespoon tomato purée
6 salted anchovy fillets, chopped
400ml red wine
200ml veal stock
100g peas
100g kale

For the polenta
1 litre whole milk
300g instant polenta
200ml double cream
150g Parmesan, finely grated
150g Gorgonzola
50g butter

Super-rich and indulgent, this is proper, rib-sticking winter comfort food.

1. Heat the oil in a heavy-based pan or flameproof casserole and gently fry the onions and the carrots for 5 minutes.

2. Add the veal, tomato purée and anchovies and cook for 5 minutes. Add the wine and stock, bring to the boil, then reduce the heat and simmer, covered, for at least 2 hours 30 minutes, or until the veal is very, very soft. A lot of sauce is good to accompany polenta, but you could take the lid off for the first 30–40 minutes of cooking to reduce the amount of liquid a little.

3. To make the polenta, bring the milk to the boil in a pan, add the polenta and cook, stirring continuously, for 5 minutes (always add the polenta to the hot milk and NOT the other way round) until it is thick and smooth – you don't want a gritty polenta.

4. Add the cream and cheeses, and mix well before adding the butter. (You can add more cream or milk to loosen the polenta if it is too thick when it comes to serving.)

5. Finish off the stew just before serving by adding the peas and kale, and cooking for a further 10 minutes.

6. To serve, make a cheffy smear of polenta on the plate, then serve with the veal on the top so juices run into the polenta.

Baked Duck Rigatoni

SERVES: **4-6**

1 tablespoon vegetable oil
1 onion, finely chopped
1 carrot, finely chopped
1 celery stick, finely chopped
4 garlic cloves, finely chopped
150g tomato purée
450ml red wine
450ml chicken stock
2 sprigs of rosemary, chopped
1 x 450g tin of confit duck legs, meat removed
and shredded
500g dried rigatoni pasta
250g grated mozzarella
100g Parmesan, finely grated
Salt and black pepper

To serve
Rosemary & Garlic Flatbread (see page 133)
Green salad

The rich earthy flavour of duck meat is a perfect match for the hearty tomato based sauce in this pasta bake. Using confit duck legs from a tin is a brilliant shortcut - and a totally legit one. Confit is a traditional French method of preserving meat, where cured duck legs are cooked slowly at a very low temperature resulting in beautifully tender meat. You can do this yourself at home, but if someone has already done the hard work, well, it would be rude not to go with it.

1. Heat the oil in a pan and gently fry the onion, carrot, celery and garlic for 5 minutes, until soft. Add the tomato purée and cook for 7–8 minutes until a rich red. This really releases so much tomatoey flavour.

2. Add the wine, stock and rosemary, bring to the boil, chuck in the duck and simmer until the meat is falling apart and the liquid has reduced to a rich, thick sauce, about 45 minutes to 1 hour. Add salt and pepper to taste.

3. Meanwhile, preheat the oven to 160°C fan/ 180°C/Gas 4. Cook the rigatoni in boiling, salted water until al dente, then drain. Mix the drained pasta into the duck sauce and transfer to an ovenproof dish.

4. Sprinkle the grated cheeses over the top and bake for 20–30 minutes until the cheese is golden and melted. Serve with a dressed green salad and the Rosemary & Garlic Flatbread (see overleaf).

Rosemary & Garlic
Flatbread

MAKES: **1**

250g strong white bread flour, plus extra
for dusting
1 teaspoon fast-action dried yeast
½ teaspoon fine salt
2 tablespoons olive oil
100–140ml water
1 tablespoon roughly chopped rosemary
½ teaspoon sea salt flakes
50g butter
2 garlic cloves, chopped
1 tablespoon chopped parsley

TOP TIP

This Rosemary & Garlic Flatbread is perfect to accompany the Duck Rigatoni on page 130, but you can switch up the flavourings to suit other dishes too. Try sprinkling the flatbread with sumac, a Middle Eastern spice, to add a tangy lemony accent then serve the bread alongside the Lamb Shawarma on page 123.

Homemade flatbread, still warm from the oven and slathered in garlicky butter, is one of life's simple pleasures. The active prep time needed to make the bread dough is minimal, it's the hour of proving time when the yeast works its magic that is the critical stage – and during that, you don't need to lift a finger.

1. Put the flour, yeast and fine salt into a mixing bowl and stir to combine. Add the olive oil and 100ml of the water. Use one hand to mix and bring the ingredients together. Slowly add enough of the remaining water to incorporate all the flour and form a soft, but not sticky, dough (you may not need all the water).

2. Tip the dough onto a lightly floured surface and knead for 5–10 minutes until smooth and elastic. Place in a clean bowl, cover and leave to prove for at least 1 hour, or until doubled in size.

3. Line a large baking sheet with baking parchment and preheat the oven to 200°C fan/220°C/Gas 7.

4. Tip the dough onto a lightly floured surface. Using a rolling pin, roll the dough into a circle 30cm in diameter and transfer to the lined tray. Using your fingertips, make indentations into the dough and sprinkle with the chopped rosemary and sea salt. Bake for 10 minutes.

5. Meanwhile, put the butter and garlic in a small pan and heat until the butter has melted.

6. Remove the bread from the oven and brush with the garlic butter, then return to the oven for 5 minutes until golden and cooked through. Just before serving, sprinkle with the chopped parsley.

Cola-Brined Chicken
with Waffles

For the cola-brined chicken
1.5 litres cola
1 tablespoon salt
10 thyme sprigs
4 garlic cloves
100ml hot sauce
12 bone-in chicken thighs, skin on
Vegetable oil, for deep-frying

For the flour mix
500g plain flour
1 tablespoon salt
1 tablespoon garlic powder
1 tablespoon smoked paprika
1 tablespoon dried oregano

For the waffles
90ml whole milk
7g fast-action dried yeast
8g soft light brown sugar
125g plain flour
8g polenta
120ml buttermilk
50g butter, melted
1 egg

To serve
Watermelon, cut into 5cm cubes
Maple syrup

TOP TIP

It's best to marinate the chicken for 3 hours, but when short on time even 1 hour will impart the caramel flavour of the cola all the way through.

This recipe is inspired by a dish that Simon ate when he lived in Miami (for a week). It's a lot of cola, but it gets drained away, so don't worry about consuming too much sugar.

1. For the cola brine, combine all the ingredients in a bowl and stir until the salt dissolves. Add the chicken thighs, cover and chill for at least 3 hours. (Or do this using a large zip-lock bag.)

2. To make the waffle batter, warm the milk, add the yeast and sugar and leave to bubble for 5–10 minutes.

3. Combine the flour, polenta, buttermilk, melted butter and egg in a bowl, then add the milk and yeast mixture, mix until smooth, and set aside at room temperature for 1 hour.

4. When ready to cook the chicken, bring it back to room temperature.

5. Combine all the ingredients for the flour mix. Take the chicken thighs out of the brine and pat dry. Roll in the flour mix and pat off any excess.

6. Pour enough oil for deep-frying into a deep-fryer or wide, deep pan, making sure it is no more than one-third full. Heat to 180°C, or until a cube of white bread browns in just under 1 minute.

7. Deep-fry the chicken, in batches, for about 12 minutes, turning occasionally. Drain on kitchen paper and keep warm.

8. Cook the waffles on a waffle iron for a total of 4–5 minutes, then serve the chicken with the waffles, watermelon and maple syrup.

Cuban Chicken
with Rice

SERVES: **4**

100g butter, plus extra for greasing
350g boneless chicken breast, cut into chunks
125g spicy sausage, sliced into chunks
2 carrots, sliced
1 onion, sliced
1 garlic clove, chopped
350g short-grain rice
4 tomatoes, roughly chopped
1 x 400g tin of mixed beans, rinsed and drained
1.5 litres chicken stock
3 tablespoons Cuban dark rum
1 tablespoon chopped parsley
Salt and black pepper

For the spice mix
2 teaspoons each of dried oregano, ground
cumin, paprika, garlic powder, onion powder, salt
and white pepper
2 teaspoons soft dark brown sugar
1 tablespoon vegetable oil

To serve
Chilli sauce or garlic mayo

The beans in this dish break down to make the rice deliciously sticky.

1. Preheat the oven to 160°C fan/180°C/Gas 4.

2. Mix the dry ingredients for the spice mix into the oil and set aside.

3. Melt half the butter in a large frying pan, add the chicken and fry until golden, then remove the chicken from the pan.

4. Fry the sausage, carrots, onion and garlic in the same pan until soft, then remove from the pan.

5. Mix the rice with the softened vegetables, tomatoes, mixed beans and the remaining butter. Season well with salt and pepper.

6. Put half the rice mixture in a well-buttered casserole dish, sit the chicken on top, then spoon over the rest of the rice mixture.

7. Mix the stock and rum into the spice mix and pour this over the rice. Cover and bake for about 30–45 minutes or until the rice is sticky and gooey, with no bite.

8. Sprinkle over the parsley and serve with chilli sauce or garlic mayo.

San Francisco Fish Stew

SERVES: **4**

100ml extra virgin olive oil
1 onion, finely sliced
3 garlic cloves, sliced
150ml white wine
225ml fish or chicken stock
1 x 400g tin of chopped tomatoes
1 bay leaf
A few thyme sprigs
1 tablespoon hot sauce
300g clams, cleaned and any with broken shells discarded
30g butter
300g salmon, cut into chunks
300g king prawns, shelled and deveined, tail shell left on
Handful of chopped parsley
Grated zest and juice of 1 lemon

To serve
Slices of sourdough bread
Garlic mayo

Fisherman's Wharf in San Francisco is renowned for its seafood stews, originally made by fisherman on their boats but now served in many of the local restaurants. Cooked in a tasty tomato broth spiked with white wine, this version combines clams and prawns with generous chunks of salmon, but you could use mussels and squid instead of clams and prawns or swap the salmon for whatever firm-fleshed fish looks freshest at the fishmongers.

1. Heat the oil in a pan and gently fry the onion and garlic for 5 minutes. Add the wine, bring to the boil and reduce by half.

2. Add the stock, tomatoes, bay, thyme and hot sauce and bring back up to the boil.

3. Add the clams, cover and cook for 5 minutes until their shells open.

4. Reduce to a simmer, then add the butter, salmon and prawns. Cook for 3 minutes, then add the parsley and lemon zest and juice. Serve with sourdough and garlic mayo.

Bloody Mary Lasagne

SERVES: **6-8**

450g lean minced beef
1 tablespoon vegetable oil
1 onion, finely chopped
2 garlic cloves, sliced
1 red pepper and 1 green pepper, finely chopped
150g button mushrooms, sliced
200g tomato purée
2 x 400g tins of chopped tomatoes
1 teaspoon each of dried thyme, parsley
and oregano
2 bay leaves
3 tablespoons vodka
1 tablespoon Worcestershire sauce
300g dried lasagne sheets
200g mature Cheddar, grated
75g Parmesan, grated
Salt and black pepper

For the béchamel sauce
100g butter
100g plain flour
1 litre hot milk
A pinch of nutmeg
225g Parmesan, grated

To serve
Rosemary & Garlic Flatbread (see page 133)
Green salad

A Bloody Mary is one of our favourite drinks, so we thought, why not incorporate those same flavours on the plate? The vodka lends a richness and warmth to the tomato sauce. But don't worry if you're the designated driver, all the alcohol evaporates during the cooking.

1. Fry the mince in a large non-stick pan for 8 minutes, stirring until evenly browned, then remove to a bowl.

2. In the same pan, heat the oil and gently fry the onion, garlic, peppers and mushrooms.

3. Add the mince back in, stir in the tomato purée and cook for 6 minutes. Add the tinned tomatoes, herbs, vodka and Worcestershire sauce, bring to the boil, then reduce the heat and simmer for 40 minutes. Add salt and pepper to taste.

4. Preheat the oven to 180°C fan/200°C/Gas 6.

5. For the béchamel, melt the butter in a pan, add the flour, stir to combine and cook for 2–3 minutes.

Continued overleaf →

6. Add the hot milk a little at a time, stirring constantly. When it's all been added, slowly bring to the boil, still stirring, then simmer for 2–3 minutes only. Season with salt, pepper and nutmeg and stir in the grated Parmesan.

7. To assemble, put a little béchamel in the base of a baking dish, 30 x 20cm, then add a layer of pasta sheets over that, then a layer of meat, then another layer of béchamel.

8. Repeat the layers, finishing with sauce. Sprinkle over the grated cheeses and bake for 40 minutes, until golden on top and the pasta is cooked through.

9. Serve with a dressed green salad and the Rosemary & Garlic Flatbread (see page 132).

Lamb Shanks with Pearl Barley & Red Wine

SERVES: **4**

2 tablespoons vegetable oil
4 lamb shanks
6 carrots, sliced
2 onions, sliced
3 garlic cloves, sliced
1 bay leaf
A few thyme sprigs
2 tablespoons tomato purée
25g plain flour
500ml red wine
500ml chicken stock
75g pearl barley
Salt and black pepper

To serve
Buttery mashed potato

This is a hearty dish for wholesome appetites. Lamb shanks are a great inexpensive cut of meat, but the secret to perfect results is to cook the shank low and slow until the meat falls apart. This recipe works brilliantly when cooked on the hob, but if you have a slow cooker then it will be just as good made that way.

1. Heat 1 tablespoon of the oil in a heavy-based pan or flameproof casserole and add the lamb shanks, two at a time (crowding the pan reduces the heat and steams rather than fries the lamb). Fry on all sides to get a good colour on them, then remove to a plate.

2. Add the remaining 1 tablespoon oil, then gently fry the carrots, onions, garlic, bay leaf and thyme in the pan for 5 minutes.

3. Stir in the purée and cook for 5 minutes, then add the flour and cook for 2 minutes. Gradually add the wine and stock, stirring to make a smooth sauce, then bring to the boil.

4. Turn down to a simmer and add the lamb back to the pan, with the pearl barley. Add plenty of salt and pepper to taste, cover and cook over a low heat for 3 hours, until the meat pulls easily away from the bone. Serve with buttery mash.

Images overleaf →

Bean Bourguignon

SERVES: **4-6**

Olive oil, for frying
1 onion, finely sliced
2 x 400g tins of mixed beans (such as butter and
cannellini), drained and washed
1 tablespoon plain flour
1 bottle red burgundy
250ml vegetable stock
1 garlic clove, peeled and sliced
1 sprig each of thyme and parsley
1 bay leaf
100g smoked tofu, cubed
250g chestnut mushrooms, sliced
100g green beans, halved

To serve
Steamed rice
Chopped parsley

A hearty, cold weather, comfort blanket of a dish, this slow-simmered stew uses only a handful of ingredients but gets its rich and deep taste from cooking for an hour on a low heat. Happily, the majority of the cooking time is 'hands-off'. Like any stew this bean bourguignon gets even better after a couple of days once the flavours have truly melded, so make enough for leftovers.

1. Heat the oil in a heavy-based pan or flameproof casserole and gently fry the onions for 8 minutes. Add the mixed beans, sprinkle over the flour and mix well.

2. Pour in the wine and stock and stir to combine. Add the garlic, thyme, parsley and bay leaf, then cover with a lid and leave to simmer for 1 hour.

3. In a separate pan, fry the tofu and mushrooms. Add to the casserole with the green beans and cook for another 5 minutes.

4. Serve with steamed rice and chopped parsley.

Squash with Pistachio Pesto

SERVES: **6-8**

5 tablespoons olive oil
125ml runny honey
5 tablespoons sherry vinegar
3 garlic cloves, sliced
3 or 4 thyme sprigs
Salt and pepper
1 butternut squash, cut into wedges

For the pesto
50g pistachios, shelled
50g Parmesan-style vegetarian cheese
100ml extra virgin olive oil
25g each of mint, dill and parsley

To serve
Greek yoghurt
Pomegranate seeds
Lemon juice

Pesto is super simple to make yourself at home and the results are far, far tastier than anything you can buy in a store. We urge you to try it once - we promise, you won't go back to the bottled. Using pistachios rather than the traditional pine nuts to make pesto instantly gives it a Middle Eastern slant. Drizzle the pesto over squash that has been roasted until the edges are nicely caramelised and then scatter over some vibrant pomegranate seeds, which bring a burst of acidity to contrast the sweet squash.

1. Preheat the oven to 180°C fan/200°C/Gas 6.

2. Combine the olive oil, honey, sherry vinegar, garlic, thyme, salt and pepper in a bowl. Add the butternut squash wedges and turn to coat.

3. Spread the coated butternut squash wedges over a roasting tray and place in the hot oven for around 35 minutes, or until soft and slightly charred.

4. Meanwhile make the pesto. In a food processor, blitz the pistachios and vegetarian cheese until coarsely ground. Next, add the olive oil and herbs and blitz again.

5. Arrange the butternut squash wedges on to serving plates, and then top with a spoonful of Greek yoghurt. Drizzle over a generous amount of the pistachio pesto and a scattering of pomegranate seeds. Serve with a drizzle of lemon juice.

Sometimes it's worth taking your time over preparing a drink, especially when the rewards reaped are the most delicious cocktail to be sipped and savoured. Cheers!

Carl Brown's Pink Pepper Gin Cup

SERVES: **1**

For the pink pepper mix
500ml pink pepper gin
Zest and juice of 1 pink grapefruit
400g strawberries
1 teaspoon vanilla extract
Cardamom tea
300g sugar
400ml water

For the cocktail
50ml pink pepper mix (see above)
Bitter lemon, to top up
Strawberry, to garnish
Grapefruit slice, to garnish

1. To make the pink pepper mix, combine all the ingredients in a jar. Leave it to macerate for a week, shaking the jar every day to mix.

2. To make the cocktail, strain the pink pepper mix to remove the strawberries and other solids.

3. Fill a glass with ice and pour the pink pepper mix into the glass over the ice.

4. Top up the glass with bitter lemon.

5. Garnish with a sliced strawberry and a slice of grapefuit.

Karina Elias's Beet Bourbon Sour

SERVES: **1**

For the spiced beet bourbon infusion
4 raw beetroots
1 bottle of bourbon (such as Jim Beam)
5 cloves
3 star anise
3 cinnamon stick
10 black peppercorns
10 strips of orange peel
1 teaspoon ground nutmeg

For the cocktail
50ml spiced beet bourbon infusion (see above)
15ml sugar syrup
15ml freshly squeezed lemon juice
2 dashes of Angostura bitters

1. Place the beetroot in a large pan of water. Bring to the boil and then lower the heat and simmer for 35–40 minutes, or until soft.

2. Pour the bourbon into a separate pan and add the cloves, star anise, cinnamon stick, peppercorns, orange peel and nutmeg. Add the cooked beetroot and leave to infuse overnight.

3. Pour all the cocktail ingredients into a cocktail shaker and shake hard.

4. Place an oversized ice cube into a short tumbler. Strain the contents of the shaker into the glass.

Neil Ridley & Joel Harrison's Mulled Chocolate Cider

SERVES: **10**

3 litres dry English cider (such as Thatcher's Vintage)
Peel of 1 orange and 1 lemon
100g unrefined muscovado sugar
200ml American bourbon whiskey (such as
  Four Roses, Bulleit or Maker's Mark)
100g dark chocolate (minimum 70% cocoa)
Gold leaf, to garnish

For the spice bag
2 vanilla pods, split
1 tablespoon pink peppercorns
4 star anise
2 fresh bay leaves
2 cinnamon sticks
2 teaspoons cloves
1 teaspoon cardamom pods

1. Place all the spices in a muslin bag and tie the opening tightly to secure.

2. Pour the cider into a large pan, then add the spice bag, citrus peels and sugar.

3. Bring the contents of the pan to a light boil, then turn the heat down to low and simmer for a further 15 minutes.

4. Remove the pan from the heat and add the rum.

5. Break the chocolate into small pieces and set aside one piece to garnish each drink. Add the rest of the chocolate to the pan. Whisk together until the chocolate has melted.

6. Transfer the mulled cider to a punchbowl, ready to serve in silver goblets.

7. Garnish each drink with a piece of reserved chocolate and a tiny piece of gold leaf, if using.

Ian Burrell's Buttered Rum Fashion

SERVES: **1**

For the brown butter rum
1 x 700ml bottle rum (such as Gold Barbados)
125g butter

For the cocktail (per drink)
60ml brown butter rum (see above)
1 dash of vanilla essence
3 dashes of chocolate bitters
1 tablespoon soft demerara sugar
Chocolate raisin, to garnish

1. To make the brown butter rum, melt the butter in a pan. Continue warming the butter to remove any water – it will sizzle and pop – tilting the pan to avoid the butter burning. When the butter turns amber and smells nutty, remove from the heat. Leave to cool until tepid.

2. Pour the rum into an airtight jar. Add the brown butter, then close the jar. Shake the jar to mix the rum and butter. Chill for 3 days.

3. After 3 days in the fridge, the butter in the jar will have solidified. To separate the hard butter and the rum, place the jar in a bowl of warm water.

4. Strain the buttered rum through a muslin cloth and discard the butter solids. Transfer the rum to a bottle and refrigerate until needed.

5. To make the cocktail, place a large ice cube into a cocktail shaker and pour in the brown butter rum. Add the vanilla essence, chocolate bitters and sugar. Stir until the sugar has dissolved.

6. Place a large ice cube into a rocks glass and strain the contents of the shaker into the glass over the ice. Garnish with a chocolate raisin.

super

super

super

super

tasty

Some of the recipes that we've cooked on the show
are so good that we've just had to include them in
this book. For that reason we've created a 'catch-all'
chapter to highlight some of the punchiest, most
full-flavoured recipes that we've ever cooked…
plus a few new ones too.

What makes a supertasty plate of food? Well, it's the
same chemistry that makes a successful show on a
Sunday. The best individual ingredients that meld
together to make a memorable whole that is often
greater than the sum of its parts. But there's always
room for the unexpected!

Shredded Chicken & Charred Avo Salad

SERVES: **6**

1 lemon, quartered
3 garlic cloves
1 chicken, about 1.5kg
1 onion, sliced
30g butter
200ml chicken stock
Salt and black pepper

For the dressing
Juice of 1 lemon
10g sugar
10g sea salt
150ml extra virgin olive oil

For the salad
3 avocados, halved, stoned and peeled
A little olive oil
200g cooked barley (150g uncooked weight)
2 x 400g tins of chickpeas, drained and rinsed
6 spring onions, sliced
1 cucumber, diced
Handful each of mint and parsley, chopped

To serve
Warm bread

There's no meat we will not shred in the quest to find the tastiest dishes known to man.

1. Preheat the oven to 160°C fan/180°C/Gas 4.

2. Put the lemon and garlic inside the chicken cavity and season well. Put the sliced onion in a layer in the bottom of a roasting dish and dot the butter over the top. Add the stock and sit the chicken on top, then cover loosely with foil and roast for 45 minutes. Remove the foil and roast for 45 minutes more.

3. Remove from the oven, leave until cool enough to handle, then shred the meat into the liquid in the dish. Squeeze the lemon juice and garlic in there too. Discard the bones.

4. Mix the dressing ingredients together and leave to stand for 5 minutes before using.

5. Brush a little oil on the cut side of the avocados, then fry on the cut side for 2–3 minutes in a frying pan, until charred.

6. Mix the barley, chickpeas, spring onion, cucumber and herbs, and coat well in the dressing.

7. Spoon the barley mixture onto a serving platter, add the shredded chicken and the avocado halves, and serve with warm bread.

Chicken Thighs with Mole Sauce & Green Rice

SERVES: **6**

18 boneless chicken thighs (skin on)
2 tablespoons vegetable oil
Salt and black pepper

For the mole sauce
2 dried ancho chillies
3 slices of white bread, toasted
500ml chicken stock
8 plum tomatoes, halved
1 tablespoon vegetable oil
1 onion, diced
2 fresh red chillies
1 teaspoon chilli flakes
50g flaked almonds
2 tablespoons ground cumin
1 teaspoon dried thyme
4 cloves
4 allspice berries
1 cinnamon stick
125g dark chocolate (minimum 70% cocoa solids), grated
1 tablespoon raisins

For the green rice
1 tablespoon vegetable oil
4 spring onions, chopped
1 garlic clove, chopped
200g jasmine rice
450ml chicken stock
50g peas
50g butter
70g spinach
Bunch of coriander
3 tablespoons white wine vinegar

Rich, dark and delicious, mole is a signature sauce in Mexican cooking. There are many variations, but the basic ingredients include plenty of chillies and a touch of chocolate to tame the heat of the chillies. The dried ancho chillies here add a wonderful smokiness.

1. To make the mole sauce, soak the dried ancho chillies and toasted bread in stock for 5 minutes.

2. Add the tomatoes to a frying pan and dry-fry until blackened all over. Remove to a plate.

3. Heat the oil in the pan and fry the onion for 5 minutes. Add the remaining sauce ingredients, with the tomatoes, soaked bread and chillies, along with the soaking stock. Bring to the boil and simmer for 8 minutes. Remove the spices and blend the sauce until smooth. Keep warm.

4. To make the rice, heat the oil in a pan over a low heat, add the spring onions and garlic and gently fry for 5 minutes. Add the rice, stir well, then add the stock, bring to the boil, cover and simmer for 15 minutes. Take off the heat, stir in the peas and butter, and leave to stand for 5 minutes.

5. In a food processor, blend the spinach, coriander and vinegar, then stir through the rice.

6. While the rice is cooking, preheat the oven to 160°C fan/180°C/Gas 4. Season the chicken well, heat the oil in a frying pan and fry the chicken for 5 minutes until nicely golden. Transfer to an oven dish and bake for 20 minutes.

7. Serve the chicken with the green rice and mole sauce, as well as sour cream, coriander and lime wedges, if preferred.

Williamsburg Hipster Chicken with Sweet Potato Salad

SERVES: **4**

4 boneless, skinless chicken breasts
4 sweet potatoes, about 600g, left unpeeled
and cut into chunks
1 teaspoon chilli flakes
2 tablespoons olive oil
1 red onion, halved and sliced into half-moons
150g tinned black beans (drained weight), rinsed
100g kale
Salt and black pepper

For the marinade
60g mint leaves
60g oregano leaves
60g parsley leaves
60g coriander leaves
1 garlic clove, chopped
4 tablespoons lemon juice
150ml olive oil
175ml white wine
1 teaspoon ground cumin
1 teaspoon sea salt
1 teaspoon freshly ground black pepper

Sweet potato? Tick. Black beans? Tick. Kale? Tick. On the roster of hipster ingredients, this chicken dish ticks a lot of superfood boxes. It's just missing an avocado and a few chia seeds… but that would just be plain weird. Instead, the herby marinated chicken pairs beautifully with the warm sweet potato salad that combines the contrasting heat of chilli flakes and coolness of sour cream. Bashing the chicken breasts until they are flat and thin not only gives a wider surface area for the marinade to penetrate the meat, but it also means they are super-quick to cook in the oven.

1. Put all the marinade ingredients in a food processor and blitz until smooth. Place the chicken breasts between 2 sheets of clingfilm or baking parchment and bash them out with a rolling pin until thin.

2. Put the chicken in an oven dish, coat with the marinade, cover and refrigerate for 24 hours.

3. Preheat the oven to 180°C fan/200°C/Gas 6. Remove the chicken from the fridge to return to room temperature.

4. Put the sweet potato chunks in a roasting tin or dish and add the chilli flakes, olive oil and plenty of salt and pepper. Toss to coat, then roast for about 25 minutes on the top shelf of the oven, until lightly charred and cooked through.

5. After 10 minutes, remove the cover from the chicken and cook below the sweet potatoes in the oven for 15 minutes.

6. Meanwhile, put the onion, black beans and kale in a bowl. Mix the dressing ingredients together and toss through the salad ingredients.

7. Serve the chicken in wide slices with the marinade spooned over, with the sweet potatoes and salad alongside.

For the dressing
1 garlic clove, grated
4 tablespoons mayonnaise
3 tablespoons sour cream
1 tablespoon English mustard
2 tablespoons red wine vinegar

Chicken & Rabbit Pie

SERVES: **6**

For the pastry
450g plain flour
50ml milk
50ml water
150g lard, diced
1 egg yolk, beaten
Salt and black pepper

For the filling
500g chicken breast fillets, cut into cubes
450g pork sausage meat
400g boneless rabbit meat, chopped
60g dried apricots, chopped
1 teaspoon freshly ground nutmeg
1 teaspoon ground allspice
1 tablespoon finely chopped rosemary
3 tablespoons Worcestershire sauce
Generous pinch each of salt and ground white pepper

To serve
Pickled walnuts
Salad leaves

TOP TIP

This pie is even tastier the day after making… if it hangs around that long. Treat it just like you would a pork pie and keep it in the fridge, then let it come back to room temperature before serving.

Rabbit is an underused meat, despite being beautifully lean and incredibly tasty. A good old-fashioned pie is one of the best ways to cook with rabbit. In this pie filling, the gamey taste of the rabbit is sweetened by dried apricots and enlivened by nutmeg and allspice.

1. Preheat the oven to 160°C fan/180°C/Gas 4.

2. To make the pastry, sift the flour into a bowl and season well.

3. Warm the milk, water and lard together in a pan until the lard has melted. Bring just to the boil then pour onto the flour mix. Stir well to make a dough, then turn out onto a floured surface and knead for 3–4 minutes.

4. Save enough dough for a lid (about a third). Roll the remaining dough out, then press into the base and sides of a 20cm loose-based tin. If it's a bit difficult to roll, just press it into the tin.

5. To make the filling, place everything in a large bowl and mix well, then spoon into the pastry case, pressing the mixture down.

6. Roll out the reserved piece of pastry into a round that will fit over the pie as a lid. Brush beaten egg yolk around the rim of the pastry case, add the lid and press gently around the edges to seal.

7. Brush the top with beaten egg yolk, cut a hole in the middle for steam to escape and bake for about 1 hour.

8. Allow to cool completely, still in the tin. Serve cold, in big slices with pickled walnuts and salad.

Chicken Katsu Curry Burger

SERVES: **4**

100g plain flour
2 teaspoons salt
2 tablespoons curry powder
3 eggs
200g panko breadcrumbs
2 boneless, skinless chicken breasts, cut into
about 5 goujons per breast
Vegetable oil, for deep-frying

For the curry sauce
1–2 tablespoons vegetable oil
1 onion, diced
1 garlic clove, chopped
2 carrots, chopped
1 tablespoon plain flour
2 tablespoons curry powder
750ml chicken stock
2 tablespoons honey
2 tablespoons light soy sauce
2 teaspoons garam masala
1 teaspoon cornflour mixed to a paste with
2 tablespoons water

To assemble
4 tablespoons mayonnaise
4 brioche buns, toasted
4 thin slices of red onion
4 leaves of butter lettuce

To serve
Sweet potato fries

We may be a bit hazy as to why this popular Japanese dish is called a curry when we all associate curries with Indian (and that's even after our food expert, Rebecca Seal, tried to educate us as to its origins). However, there is one thing we are confident about – the chicken katsu curry burger is a winner. One weekend, Simon put it on the menu at his pub as a special. It's been a fixture on the menu ever since. This is proper food.

1. Heat the oil for the sauce in a pan and cook the onion, garlic and carrots for 12 minutes over a medium heat, to soften and caramelise.

2. Add the flour and curry powder and cook for 3 minutes. Gradually add the stock, mixing until smooth after each addition. Add the honey and soy, bring to a boil, then add the garam masala and simmer for 20 minutes. Transfer to a blender and process until really smooth.

3. Put back into the pan, add the cornflour paste and simmer for 5 minutes, until thickened.

4. Mix the flour with the salt and curry powder, beat the eggs in a bowl and spread the panko breadcrumbs out on a plate.

Continued overleaf →

Never overcrowd the pan when deep-frying in hot oil. If you add too many pieces of the chicken all at once, the temperature of the oil will drop and you risk ending up with chicken that isn't as deliciously crisp as it should be. Cook the chicken goujons in small batches. You can always keep the first batches warm in the oven whilst you finish frying the rest.

5. Dip the chicken goujons first in the flour, then the egg, then the breadcrumbs.

6. Pour enough oil for deep-frying into a deep-fryer or deep pan, making sure it is no more than one-third full. Heat to 180°C, or until a cube of bread browns in just under 1 minute.

7. Add the goujons in batches and deep-fry for 6 minutes, then remove with a slotted spoon and drain on kitchen paper.

8. To serve, spread a tablespoonful of mayo on the base of each bun, add onion, then lettuce, then chicken goujons, then a good spoonful of curry sauce.

9. Put the lid on and serve with sweet potato fries, with a dish of extra sauce to dip into.

Beef Koftas

For the koftas
900g minced beef
200g fine breadcrumbs
1 garlic clove, finely chopped
1 tablespoon chopped parsley
1 tablespoon chopped mint
1 tablespoon harissa paste
1 tablespoon sumac
1 teaspoon ground cinnamon
Splash of rose water
Grated zest and juice of 2 lemons
2 egg yolks
Oil, for brushing
Salt and black pepper

For the tabbouleh
80g cooked bulgar wheat (40g uncooked)
50g parsley, chopped
50g mint, chopped
200g tomatoes, deseeded and chopped
3 spring onions, chopped
1 cucumber, diced
Grated zest and juice of 1 lemon
5 tablespoons extra virgin olive oil
1 teaspoon sumac

To serve
Flatbreads, warmed
Greek yoghurt or labneh
Pickled chillies

The key to these beef koftas is to make sure that the meat is sticky enough to hold together on the skewers, so don't use any beef mince that is too lean – you need a bit of fat to help keep this kofta moist and together. We've cooked these koftas under the grill, which works beautifully, but when they are grilled over a barbecue they become next-level nosh.

1. To make the koftas, mix all the ingredients together except the oil, with plenty of salt and pepper, then divide into 150g pieces and roll each into a ball.

2. Wet your hands and press each ball around a metal skewer to form a sausage shape about 10–12cm long. Chill for 20 minutes.

3. To make the tabbouleh, simply mix all the ingredients together except the sumac, and season well. Sprinkle over the sumac before serving.

4. Preheat the grill to hot, then brush the koftas with a little oil and grill for 8–12 minutes, turning occasionally, until golden brown all over and cooked through.

5. Serve the koftas and tabbouleh with warm flatbreads and thick yoghurt, and a few pickled green or red chillies.

Veal Chop Milanese with Salsa Verde

SERVES: **4**

4 British rose veal chops, each 175–200g
100g plain flour
200g breadcrumbs
100g Parmesan, finely grated
3 eggs
Oil and butter, for frying
Salt and black pepper

For the salsa verde
1 bunch of flat-leaf parsley
Handful of mint leaves
1 tablespoon tarragon leaves
1 tablespoon capers
15g anchovies in oil
1 tablespoon Dijon mustard
Plenty of olive oil

To serve
Sautéed spuds
Lemon halves, charred in the pan

The tenderest of veal cutlets are pounded until paper thin, then dredged in egg and covered in a nubbly coating of breadcrumbs before being fried in butter. Served with a zingy salsa verde, this dish is only ever going to be 100% delicious.

1. For the salsa verde, put the herbs, capers, anchovies and mustard into a food processor and add enough oil to blend together, until combined but still with some texture.

2. Put the veal chops between 2 sheets of clingfilm and bash with a rolling pin until thin.

3. Add salt and pepper to the flour and mix well. Mix the breadcrumbs and Parmesan together and spread out on a plate. Beat the eggs in a shallow bowl or dish.

4. Dip each chop first in the seasoned flour, then the beaten egg, then the breadcrumb mixture, to coat.

5. Heat a mixture of oil and butter in a large frying pan and fry the chops for 3–4 minutes on each side, in batches if necessary to avoid overcrowding the pan.

6. Serve the vela chops with charred lemon halves for squeezing over, the salsa verde and sautéed potatoes.

Duck Meatballs

SERVES: **4**

Vegetable oil, for frying
50g shiitake mushrooms, sliced
2 confit duck legs (from a tin is fine)
2 skinless duck breasts, chopped
125g breadcrumbs
1 egg
1 garlic clove, finely chopped
1 tablespoon chopped parsley
Salt and black pepper
Rocket leaves, to serve

For the sauce
2 shallots, finely diced
1 garlic clove, grated
2.5cm piece of fresh ginger, cut into matchsticks
200ml plum sauce
200ml chicken stock
1 teaspoon chilli flakes

Serve these duck meatballs alongside bowls of the Chinese-inspired dipping sauce and encourage everyone to dunk before they eat.

1. Heat a little oil in a frying pan, add the sliced mushrooms and cook very briefly.

2. Remove the meat from the confit dug legs and put into a food processor. Pulse until smooth-ish then pop into a bowl. Pulse the duck breast meat in the same way, and add to the bowl.

3. Add the breadcrumbs, egg, garlic, parsley, mushrooms and some salt and pepper, and mix well to combine. Roll the mixture into meatballs, about 12 in total.

4. Heat some oil in a frying pan over a medium heat, add the meatballs and fry on all sides for 4 minutes, to seal and brown.

5. To make the sauce, heat a little more oil in a clean pan and gently fry the shallots, garlic and ginger for 5 minutes. Add the plum sauce, stock and chilli flakes, bring to the boil and simmer for 5 minutes. Add the meatballs to the sauce and simmer for another 5 minutes.

6. Serve the meatballs with the sauce in a dish on the side, for dipping, and some rocket.

Spinach & Feta Tart

SERVES: **6**

Vegetable oil, for frying
1 leek, thinly sliced
1 garlic clove, chopped
100g spinach
75g rocket, plus extra to serve
150g ricotta
150g feta, crumbled
30g fresh oregano leaves
Grated zest of 1 lemon
9 eggs
100ml buttermilk
8 sheets of filo pastry
75g butter, melted

To serve
Tomato chutney

Spinach and feta is a failsafe combo. Here they work together to create a gorgeous vegetarian tart.

1. Preheat the oven to 160°C fan/180°C/Gas 4.

2. Heat a little oil in a frying pan and gently fry the leek and garlic for 6 minutes.

3. Add the spinach and rocket and cook for 2 minutes. Strain the mixture through a sieve to remove any liquid, then transfer to a bowl and add the ricotta, feta, oregano and lemon zest; mix well.

4. Beat 3 of the eggs into the buttermilk and add to the mixture in the bowl.

5. Lay a sheet of filo in a 20 x 30cm rectangular tart tin, letting it overhang.

6. Brush with melted butter and repeat until all the sheets are used up.

7. Spoon in the filling mixture and make 6 evenly spaced indentations into the filling, using the back of a spoon. Crack an egg into each space and brush the remaining butter onto the scrunched pastry edge.

8. Bake for 25 minutes, or until the eggs are set and the pastry is crisp and browned. Serve with tomato chutney and extra rocket leaves.

Miso-Glazed Gnocchi with Chestnut Mushrooms

SERVES: **4**

For the gnocchi
600g floury potatoes (such as Maris Piper or King Edward), unpeeled
1 large egg
200g plain flour
75g butter

For the mushrooms
1 onion, finely diced
2 garlic cloves, finely chopped
2 tablespoons sunflower oil
350g chestnut mushrooms, thickly sliced
1 tablespoon white miso paste
1 tablespoon light soy sauce
1 tablespoon sake (optional)
2 teaspoons rice vinegar
100g walnuts, toasted in a moderate oven for 10 minutes, then chopped
Salt and black pepper

To serve
Lamb's lettuce

With the miso and mushrooms, this dish is an umami double-whammy.

1. Boil the potatoes in salted water for 30–40 minutes, until completely tender. Drain, and when cool enough to handle, pass through a ricer into a bowl.

2. Make a well in the centre of the potato and add the egg and some salt and pepper. Add the flour, mix to form a dough, then knead for a few minutes until dry to the touch.

3. Divide the mixture evenly into three, then roll out each piece into a 2cm-diameter rope. Cut each rope into pieces at 2.5cm intervals.

4. Bring a large pan of water to the boil, and melt 50g of the butter in a large frying pan.

5. Drop the gnocchi into the boiling water, and when they rise to the top, scoop out with a slotted spoon and fry in the butter until crisp.

6. In a separate frying pan, fry the onion and garlic in the oil for 6 minutes, until softened. Remove from the pan and set aside, keeping the oil in the pan.

7. Add the remaining butter to the onion pan. Add the mushrooms and fry for 3 minutes until golden, then return the onions to the pan.

8. Mix the miso, soy and sake, if using, together in a bowl then add the mixture to the pan and cook for 3 minutes before adding the vinegar.

9. Add everything to the gnocchi and fold through to coat. Top with the chopped walnuts and serve with lamb's lettuce.

Lancashire Cheese Pie

A true northern treat, this hearty pie recipe has been passed down through the generations of my family – it's a Rimmer family classic. Creamy Lancashire cheese is a must – don't even think about using anything else.

SERVES: **4**

For the pastry
300g plain flour
150g cold butter, diced
1 teaspoon sea salt
1 tablespoon white wine vinegar
2–3 tablespoons cold water
1 egg, beaten, to glaze

For the filling
4 onions, diced
1 garlic clove, sliced
200ml water
50g butter
400g potatoes
275g mature Lancashire cheese
(Mrs Kirkham's), grated
100ml double cream
Salt and black pepper

1. For the filling, put the onions, garlic, water and butter in a pan. Cover and simmer over a low heat for 20 minutes. Remove the lid and continue cooking over a low heat until most of the liquid has evaporated. Season well and cool completely.

2. While the onion mixture is simmering, cook the potatoes in boiling, salted water until tender, then drain, cool and slice. Mix the cooled potatoes with the onion mixture and add the grated cheese and cream. Season well and set aside.

3. Meanwhile, for the pastry, rub the flour and butter together until the mixture resembles breadcrumbs, then stir through the salt.

4. Add the vinegar and enough water to bring it into a dough. Wrap and chill for 20 minutes.

5. Preheat the oven to 160°C fan/180°C/Gas 4.

6. Divide the pastry into two pieces, one double the size of the other (so two-thirds and one-third).

7. Roll out the bigger piece to a circle big enough to line a deep 20cm pie dish, and spoon the filling into the pastry-lined dish.

8. Roll out the other piece of pastry to make a lid, then place on top, crimp the edges to seal, and brush with the beaten egg.

9. Bake in the oven for 45 minutes until golden, then serve with a tomato and rocket salad.

Aubergine Chilli Tamale Pie

SERVES: **4-6**

2 aubergines, cut into big chunks
Vegetable oil, for cooking
1 onion, diced
1 garlic clove, sliced
1 green pepper, diced
250g chestnut mushrooms, sliced
1 x 400g tin of black beans, drained and rinsed
225g tinned, drained sweetcorn
225g tomato passata
300ml vegetable stock
1 tablespoon chilli powder
1 tablespoon smoked paprika
1 teaspoon cumin
75g Parmesan, finely grated
Salt and black pepper

For the topping
150g fast-cook polenta
1 tablespoon plain flour
1 tablespoon sugar
1 teaspoon baking powder
1 egg, beaten
2 teaspoons vegetable oil
About 150ml milk
6 finely chopped jalapeños (from a jar)

To serve
Sour cream
Coriander leaves
Lime wedges

American comfort food at its best, this is a real crowdpleaser. Instead of the usual beef chilli, the spicy filling is made with aubergines.

1. Put the aubergine in a bowl, add 4 tablespoons oil and toss to coat. Season well, then cook in a griddle pan until charred and soft. Set aside.

2. Heat 2 tablespoons oil in a pan and gently fry the onion, garlic and pepper for 5 minutes.

3. Add the mushrooms and cook for 5 minutes. Add everything except the Parmesan, bring to the boil and simmer for 15 minutes. Meanwhile, preheat the oven to 160°C fan/180°C/Gas 4.

4. Stir the aubergine into the filling mixture, season well then spoon into an ovenproof dish.

5. Mix the polenta, flour, sugar and baking powder in a bowl. Add the beaten egg and oil to the dry ingredients, then stir in enough milk to make a soft, not runny batter. Add the jalapeños.

6. Spoon the topping over the aubergine filling, sprinkle over the Parmesan and bake for about 25 minutes, until golden. Serve with sour cream, coriander and lime wedges.

Rosemary Skewered Monkfish
on Pearl Barley Risotto

SERVES: **3-4**

100ml olive oil
Grated zest and juice of 1 lemon
3-4 monkfish tail fillets, each 150–200g, fully trimmed (remove membrane and sinew)
4 long sprigs of rosemary
150g cooking chorizo, cut into 1cm cubes
1 onion, finely chopped
1 garlic clove, finely chopped
500ml fish stock
250g pearl barley
100g frozen peas
Salt and black pepper

For even more flavour, cook these monkfish skewers over charcoal to get good colour on the fish and a wonderful amount of charring. Fish and meat always taste that much better when cooked over a flame. Using pearl barley in the risotto, instead of the usual rice, gives a nutty flavour and chewy texture.

1. Mix the olive oil and lemon zest and juice in a dish or bowl, add the monkfish, season and set aside for at least 20 minutes.

2. Strip the leaves off the main stem of the rosemary sprigs (reserve until later), leaving the top leaves intact. Pierce a hole in the base of each fish fillet and push a skewer right through.

3. Fry the chorizo in a pan until crispy, then remove. Add the onion and garlic to the pan with the chorizo oil, then add enough of the stock to cover. Cook until just soft.

Continued overleaf →

4. Add the pearl barley, season and add a ladleful of stock. When it has all been absorbed, add more stock. Keep adding stock in this way.

5. When the barley is three-quarters cooked (the grain has swollen but the centre still has bite) add the chorizo back in, then stir in the peas.

6. Finely chop the reserved rosemary leaves and add to the risotto.

7. Meanwhile, chargrill the fish in a grill pan or on a barbecue for about 8 minutes, turning occasionally so that it colours on the outside, and is firm to the touch but not rubbery.

8. Serve the risotto with the monkfish skewers on top and charred lemon halves to squeeze over the fish.

Cauli Tikka Kebab

SERVES: **6**

800g cauliflower, cut into florets
2 red peppers, cut neatly into 3cm cubes
Juice of 1 lime
100g butter, melted
Natural yoghurt, to drizzle

For the marinade
100ml natural yoghurt
Juice of 1 lime
2 garlic cloves, crushed
2.5cm piece of fresh ginger, finely chopped
1 tablespoon ground coriander
1 teaspoon ground cumin
1 teaspoon garam masala
1 teaspoon paprika
1 teaspoon salt

If there is such a thing as an 'It' vegetable, then it has to be the cauliflower. This is a take on Tandoori Gobi, one the of tastiest dishes that appear on the menu of most high-street Indian restaurants. It's one of our favourite vegetarian dishes.

1. Blanch the cauliflower florets in boiling water for 10 seconds, then drain and plunge into iced water, then drain again when cool.

2. Combine the marinade ingredients and coat the drained cauliflower in the marinade, then cover and chill for at least 2 hours.

3. Meanwhile, for the naan, put the yeast, sugar and 50ml of the warm water in a bowl, mix well and leave for 2 minutes.

4. Add the yoghurt, make a well in centre, then add the flour, salt and the remaining water and mix well. Knead for 5 minutes, then replace the dough in the bowl, cover and leave to prove for at least 1 hour.

5. Mix all the salsa ingredients together and set aside.

6. When ready to cook, thread the cauliflower florets onto skewers, alternating with the red pepper cubes. Mix the lime juice into the melted butter and have ready. Place the skewers under a hot grill for about 10 minutes, turning and basting with the lime and butter mixture.

For the naan
1½ teaspoons fast-action dried yeast
1 teaspoon sugar
150ml warm water
70ml natural yoghurt
300g strong white bread flour
1 teaspoon salt
2 tablespoons melted butter
1 tablespoon nigella seeds

For the salsa
2 red peppers, diced
½ red onion, diced
1 cucumber, halved, deseeded and diced
1 Scotch bonnet chilli, diced
1 mango, peeled and diced
Grated zest and juice of 2 limes
25g mint leaves, chopped
25g coriander leaves, chopped

7. Remove the naan dough to a work surface, give it a knead and divide into 6 evenly sized pieces. Roll each into a long naan shape and heat a non-stick frying pan until hot.

8. Dry-fry the naans one at a time for 3 minutes on each side, until golden and blistered in places. Keep them warm under a tea towel or in a low oven while you cook the rest.

9. To serve, brush the naans with the melted butter and sprinkle 1 teaspoon nigella seeds over each. Sit a cauliflower kebab on each, then top with the salsa and drizzle some yoghurt over the top.

Cod & Artichokes

250g butter, softened
1 garlic clove, crushed
100g sun-dried tomatoes in oil
400g cod loin
50g plain flour, seasoned with ½ teaspoon salt
and ½ teaspoon white pepper
Juice of 1 lemon
300g baby new potatoes, cooked
Good handful of cherry tomatoes, halved
200g artichoke hearts (preferably the posh
charred ones from a jar)
Plenty of chopped parsley
Salt and black pepper

One of our long-running debates is over which fish should take the crown and be declared the King of Fish. Tim maintains that cod is the rightful winner, as it is the people's fish. In this Mediterranean-inspired one-pan dish, cod goujons are cooked in a sun-dried tomato flavoured butter, mixed with baby spuds, cherry tomatoes and artichokes. It is summer in a pan.

1. Blitz the softened butter in a food processor with the garlic, sun-dried tomatoes and some pepper until smooth. Scoop into a sausage shape, wrap in greaseproof paper and chill, ideally overnight.

2. Preheat the oven to 180°C fan/200°C/Gas 6.

3. Cut the fish into goujons, then dredge in the seasoned flour.

4. Melt a good piece of the flavoured butter in a large ovenproof frying pan (keep any leftover in the freezer for future use) and, when it bubbles up, add the fish goujons, fry for a couple of minutes, turn and brown on all sides, then squeeze a load of lemon juice over. Move the fish to one side of the pan.

5. Add the potatoes, cook for 2 minutes, then add the cherry tomatoes and cook for 2 minutes, then finally the artichokes. Season well with salt and pepper.

6. Arrange it all nicely in the pan and pop in the oven for 6 minutes to crisp up. Squeeze over more lemon juice and top with lots of parsley, then serve.

Out of all the terrific tipples we've tasted during our
drinkipoos segment on the show, these are a few of
the most memorable. Cheers!

Carl Brown's
Rosemary Martini

SERVES: **1**

10ml coffee liqueur
10ml cherry liqueur
20ml rum (such as Banks)
35ml robust red wine
1 rosemary sprig

1. Pour all the ingredients into a cocktail shaker
and add the rosemary sprig. Shake vigorously.

2. Fine strain into a coupe and serve.

Karina Elias's
Wedding Bells

SERVES: **1**

40ml bourbon (such as Van Brunt Stillhouse)
15ml Cocchi Americano
20ml Dry Orange Curacao Pierre Ferrand
3 dashes of orange bitters

1. Pour all the ingredients into a rocks glass,
stir until well mixed.

2. Add a large ice cube before serving.

Ian Burrell's Petit Passion

SERVES: **1**

50ml French agricole rhum made from sugarcane
25ml freshly squeezed lime juice
15ml passion fruit purée
3 drops of vanilla essence
Champagne, to top up

1. Chill a martini glass.

2. Fill a cocktail shaker with ice. Pour in the rum and lime juice, then add the passion fruit purée and vanilla essence. Shake hard until the drink is cold.

3. Strain the contents of the shaker into the chilled martini glass.

4. Top up the glass with Champagne.

Neil Ridley & Joel Harrison's Smoky Old Fashioned

SERVES: **1**

1 heaped teaspoon dark, thick-cut orange marmalade
2 dashes of Angostura bitters
50ml smoky, single malt whisky (such as Lagavulin Distiller's Edition, Talisker or Bowmore)
Thin strip of orange peel, to garnish
Sherry-infused cherry, to garnish

For the sherry-infused cherry garnish
Fresh cherries
Dark oloroso sherry

1. To make the cherry garnish, de-stone the cherries and then prick the fruit all over. Place in a jar and pour over some oloroso sherry. Leave to macerate for a few days until needed.

2. Spoon the marmalade into a rocks glass. Dash in the bitters and pour in a small drizzle of the whisky. Muddle and stir until mixed to a smooth consistency.

3. Fill the glass with ice, add half the remaining whisky and stir slowly until the ice starts to melt.

4. Add the rest of the whisky and more ice. Keep stirring (in between the odd taste) until you have a perfect balance of smoke, spice and sweetness.

5. Garnish with a thin strip of orange peel and a sherry-infused cherry.

top 10

We didn't choose the recipes in this Top Ten chapter. The *Sunday Brunch* viewers did. Whenever we cook a dish on the show we ask that anyone who makes the recipe that week shares a photo with us online. We're always blown away by how many viewers are inspired to get cooking after seeing a recipe onscreen. So the ten recipes in this chapter are those that have received the most hits, been cooked the most by views, and received the most positive feedback.

Every once in a while, a recipe really seems to hit the spot and becomes the one and only dish that viewers cook not just for that week but way beyond. And just occasionally a recipe goes viral and takes on near legendary status, like when Simon 'invented' pulled pork.

Beef Wellington

SERVES: **8-10**

Olive oil, for rubbing
1kg aged fillet steak
About 12 crêpes, about 20cm diameter (the
number you need will depend on the
thickness/length of the beef fillet)
350g smooth chicken liver pâté
2 x 300g packets of ready-rolled puff pastry
1 egg yolk, beaten
Salt and black pepper

For the duxelles
75g butter
2 shallots, finely diced
600g field mushrooms, very finely chopped
3–4 thyme sprigs
200ml port

To serve
Roasted potatoes
Seasonal veg
Gravy

Admittedly the ingredients needed to make this Beef Wellington are a bit spendy, but for a special occasion this dish of tender beef wrapped in crisp pastry cannot fail to impress. It might sound odd to wrap the beef in a layer of crêpes before the pastry, but they soak up the juices from the meat, stopping them running into the pastry and making it soggy.

1. Rub oil over the fillet and season, then place in a hot frying pan, turning it to seal and colour on all sides. Remove and set aside to cool.

2. For the duxelles, melt the butter in a pan, add the shallots and gently fry for 2–3 minutes, until soft.

3. Add the mushrooms and thyme and cook for 6–8 minutes, then add the port, reduce to nearly nothing and set aside to cool completely.

4. Lay the crêpes in an overlapping layer on a large piece of clingfilm, and spread the duxelles mixture evenly over them.

5. Spread the pâté all over the fillet, using a knife, then sit the fillet in the middle of the duxelles-spread crêpes. Use the clingfilm to roll and pull the duxelles and crêpes around the fillet. Seal the clingfilm well to hold in shape, and chill for at least 30 minutes.

Continued overleaf →

The cooking time here will depend on how you prefer your meat done – we always go for rare or medium-rare – but it's easy to check with a probe thermometer. And remember, a long, thin piece of beef will cook more quickly than a fat fillet.

6. Preheat the oven to 180°C fan/200°C/Gas 6.

7. Cut two pieces of pastry about 5cm longer and wider than the fillet and lay one piece on a board. Carefully unwrap the fillet and sit it in the middle of the pastry.

8. Brush egg yolk onto the pastry edges around the fillet and press the other piece of pastry on top of the fillet. Press down on the pastry edges to seal, and trim if necessary. Brush egg yolk all over the pastry.

9. Bake for about 30–45 minutes, depending on how you like your meat: when tested with a probe thermometer, for rare it will read about 50°C, medium 60°C and well-done 70°C.

10. Serve the beef wellington in thick slices, with roast potatoes, steamed broccoli or other seasonal veg, and gravy.

Tandoori Cod

SERVES: **4**

450g cod, cut into large pieces
Juice of 1 lemon

For the marinade
100g natural yoghurt
Juice of 1 lime
15g garlic, very finely chopped
2.5cm piece of fresh ginger, grated
1 teaspoon ground cumin
1 tablespoon ground coriander
1 teaspoon garam masala
½ teaspoon paprika
1 teaspoon salt

For the salad
1 mango, finely diced
1 cucumber, halved, deseeded and grated
½ red onion, finely diced
200g natural yoghurt
Juice of 1 lime
2.5cm piece of fresh ginger, grated
1 teaspoon salt
20g mint, chopped, plus extra leaves to serve
10g coriander stems, chopped, plus a few extra leaves to serve

A firm meaty fish like cod lends itself to robust Indian flavours. This tandoori cod is made with a masala blend that has a pleasant spicy warmth rather than an eye-watering heat. The fish can also be cooked over a barbecue for an extra smoky flavour.

1. Mix the marinade ingredients together in a bowl, add the pieces of cod and turn to coat well. Cover and chill for 12 hours.

2. When ready to serve, mix the salad ingredients together.

3. Heat the grill until hot and remove the cod from its marinade. Grill for 6–8 minutes, turning it occasionally and basting with lemon juice as you do.

4. Serve with the salad, with extra mint and some coriander leaves scattered over the top, perhaps with naan bread.

Cottage Pie with Cauliflower Cheese Top

SERVES: **6**

450g minced beef
1 onion, finely diced
1 carrot, finely diced
1 garlic clove, crushed
2 tablespoons tomato purée
200ml fresh strong stock (veal, game or beef)
150ml Madeira
1 tablespoon chopped parsley
Salt

For the topping
500g potatoes, cut into chunks
75g butter
250g cauliflower florets
150g crème fraîche
1 tablespoon Dijon mustard
1 egg
150g strong mature Cheddar, grated

This cottage pie and cauliflower cheese mashup epitomises the magic that happens when two of the most wonderful dishes in the world collide.

1. Fry the minced beef in a large non-stick frying pan for 8 minutes, to brown all over, then remove to a plate or bowl.

2. Add the onion, carrot and garlic to the pan, and gently fry for 8 minutes before adding back the mince with the tomato purée. Stir to mix, and cook for 6 minutes. Add the stock, Madeira and parsley, bring to the boil, then simmer for 40 minutes. Set aside to cool completely.

3. Meanwhile, boil the potatoes in salted water until tender, then drain and mash with the butter until smooth. Blanch the cauliflower florets in boiling water for 2 minutes, then drain. Preheat the oven to 180°C fan/200°C/Gas 6.

4. Beat the crème fraîche, mustard and egg together, then add the grated cheese and fold in the cauliflower.

5. Tip the cooked mince into a 20cm square baking dish and level out. Top with the mash, then spoon over the cauliflower mixture.

6. Bake in the oven for 20 minutes, then finish under a hot grill to bubble the cheese. Serve with green veggies.

Pulled Lamb Vindaloo

SERVES: **4-6**

3 onions, finely sliced into rings
6 garlic cloves, finely sliced
250ml red wine
200ml red wine vinegar
1 tablespoon finely chopped rosemary
1 tablespoon chilli flakes
3-4 tablespoons vindaloo curry paste
2kg boned lamb shoulder, most of the
outer fat removed

For the Bombay potato salad
900g baby new potatoes
1 tablespoon each of cumin seeds, coriander
seeds and black peppercorns
1 teaspoon garam masala
125g natural yoghurt
Juice of 2 limes
1 tablespoon chopped mint
1 tablespoon chopped parsley
Salt

To serve
Chapatis
Mango chutney

Proving that any meat dish is improved by being 'pulled', this slow-cooked curried lamb is torn into tender shreds to serve alongside a spicy potato salad. Wrapping the lamb in double layers of parchment and foil means the meat will steam and slow cook, keeping it moist.

1. Preheat the oven to 150°C fan/170°C/Gas 3½.

2. Lay the onion rings in a large baking dish and top with the sliced garlic. Pour the wine and vinegar over, then sprinkle over the rosemary.

3. Mix the chilli flakes into the curry paste and rub all over the lamb. Sit the lamb on top of the aromatics and cover the dish tightly with a layer of baking parchment, then a second layer of foil.

4. Roast in the oven for 3½ hours, then remove the foil and parchment and roast for another 1 hour.

5. Meanwhile, for the potato salad, cook the potatoes in boiling, salted water until just tender, then drain. Leave to cool, then cut in half.

6. While the potatoes are cooking, dry-fry the whole spices for 1–2 minutes until fragrant, then grind in a pestle and mortar or spice grinder.

7. In a bowl, mix the toasted ground spices with the garam masala, yoghurt, lime juice and herbs. Add the cooled potatoes and stir gently to coat.

8. Remove the lamb from the oven and shred the meat apart, using forks. Serve the lamb and potato salad with chapatis and mango chutney.

Juicy Lucy Burger

SERVES: **4**

800g chuck steak, coarsely ground
8 rashers of back bacon
60g Monterey Jack cheese (or Cheddar), grated
Salt and black pepper

For the sauce
200g mayonnaise
2 teaspoons Worcestershire sauce
2 teaspoons Tabasco
2 teaspoons Dijon mustard
3 roasted garlic cloves (see page 67), squeezed
from their skins

To assemble
4 brioche burger buns with sesame, cut in half
Sliced gherkins
Sliced tomato
Lettuce leaves

To serve
Fat chips

Making burgers from coarsely ground chuck steak gives them extra flavour and a meatier texture. Monterey Jack is a classic American burger cheese. With a Juicy Lucy, the cheese is placed inside the meat patty instead of on top, so that it oozes out of the burger as you take a bite. Add more or less Tabasco and Dijon mustard to the sauce, depending on how much of a kick you like.

1. For the sauce, mix all the ingredients together in a bowl.

2. Season the minced steak well and divide into 8 balls, each 100g, then press each ball out into a flat patty shape.

3. Grill the bacon until crisp, then crumble.

4. Divide the grated cheese and crumbled bacon between 4 of the meat patties, in the centre. Put the remaining patties on top and press all around the edges to seal.

5. Fry, grill or griddle the stuffed burgers for about 10 minutes, until cooked to your liking.

6. Spread some sauce on the bottom half of each burger bun and add some gherkin slices. Top with a burger, add sliced tomato and lettuce, and serve with fat chips.

Pulled Pork with Beans

SERVES: **4**

For the pork (makes enough for 8)
1 tablespoon chilli flakes
1 tablespoon wholegrain mustard
1 tablespoon finely chopped thyme
2kg pork shoulder, most of the outer fat removed
3 onions, finely sliced
6 garlic cloves, finely sliced
250ml dry cider
200ml white wine vinegar
Salt and white pepper

For the beans (serves 4)
1 tablespoon vegetable oil
1 red onion, diced
2 x 400g tins of butter beans, drained and rinsed
1 x 400g tin of kidney beans, drained and rinsed
3 tablespoons soft dark brown sugar
3 tablespoons molasses or treacle
1 tablespoon Dijon mustard
2 tablespoons tomato ketchup
3 tablespoons apple cider vinegar

For the slaw (serves 4)
¼ head of white cabbage, finely sliced
2 carrots, grated
2 red onions, sliced
1 red chilli, finely chopped
1 tablespoon smoked paprika
125g mayonnaise
3 tablespoons salad cream
Grated zest and juice of 1 lime
1 tablespoon Worcestershire sauce

This is our most downloaded recipe ever, so it was a total no-brainer when it came to selecting recipes for this chapter. Pulled pork has become synonymous with Sunday Brunch ever since Simon 'invented' it back in 2014. And its popularity never wanes. The pork shoulder is enough to serve 8, so if you're cooking for a large group double up the beans. Otherwise, you'll have leftovers of the pulled pork to make epic sarnies.

1. Preheat the oven to 150°C fan/170°C/ Gas 3½.

2. Mix the chilli, mustard and thyme together, with some salt and white pepper, and rub the mixture into the pork.

3. Put the onions and garlic into the base of a large roasting dish or tin, and sit the pork on top. Pour the cider and vinegar over, then cover the dish tightly with a sheet of baking parchment, then a layer of foil over that.

4. Roast in the oven for 3 hours, then uncover and roast for 1 hour more. Remove from the oven and shred the meat, using forks.

Continued overleaf →

5. While the pork is finishing cooking, make the slaw and cook the beans.

6. To make the slaw, mix all the ingredients together in a bowl and toss to coat.

7. To make the beans, heat the oil in a pan for the beans, add the red onion and fry for 5 minutes. Add the remaining ingredients, mix well and cook for 6 minutes.

8. Add half the pork and some of the pan juices to the beans and stir well. Serve the beans and extra shreds of pork with the slaw. Alternatively, pile the pulled pork and beans into a brioche burger bun and serve with the slaw on the side.

Butter Chicken

4 x 150g chicken breasts, diced
Lemon juice, for basting
Melted butter, for basting

For the marinade
200ml natural yoghurt
Juice of 1 lime
1 tablespoon minced garlic
2.5cm piece ginger, grated
1 teaspoon cumin
1 tablespoon ground coriander
1 teaspoon garam masala
A pinch of paprika
A pinch of salt

For the sauce
100g butter
1 onion, grated
2.5cm piece fresh ginger, grated
2 garlic cloves, crushed
100g tomato purée
2 small red chillies, finely chopped
A pinch of chilli powder
2 teaspoons garam masala
200ml water
200ml double cream
A handful of fresh coriander
Salt and black pepper

To serve
Basmati rice
Naan bread

All hail the curry, our nation's favourite dish.

1. To make the marinade, blend all the ingredients together in a non-reactive container. Add the diced chicken and toss in the marinade until well coated. Cover with clingfilm and leave to marinate in the fridge for 12 hours.

2. When ready to cook, bring the chicken to room temperature, then thread the marinated chicken pieces on to metal skewers. Place under a hot grill for 6–8 minutes, turning occasionally, and basting with lemon juice and butter.

3. To make the sauce, melt the butter in a pan and fry the onion until golden. Add the ginger and garlic and cook for 1 minute. Add the tomato purée, chillies and chilli powder, garam masala and water then cook for 2–3 minutes. Lower the heat, add the cream and cook for a further 1 minute.

4. Stir in the cooked chicken and serve on basmati rice with a scattering of coriander and a warm naan bread.

Jerk Chicken Kebabs

SERVES: **8**

900g boneless, skinless chicken thighs
2 red peppers, cut into chunks

For the jerk seasoning
1 onion
3 spring onions
1 Scotch bonnet chilli
2 garlic cloves
1 tablespoon five-spice powder
1 tablespoon all-spice berries
1 tablespoon white pepper
1 teaspoon dried thyme
1 teaspoon nutmeg
100ml light soy sauce
50ml vegetable oil

For the salsa
1 red onion, diced
1 mango, diced
1 Scotch bonnet, finely chopped
1 garlic clove, finely chopped
1 cucumber, deseeded and diced
50g coriander, chopped
Zest and juice of 2 limes

To serve
8 flatbreads
1 head of baby gem lettuce, shredded
Sour cream
Coconut shavings

This super spicy jerk seasoning enlivens any meat, but is especially good with chicken. If you prefer to barbecue your chicken, light the coals 1 hour before serving, and for a more authentic Jamaican flavour, add wood chips for smoke.

1. Mix the jerk seasoning ingredients together in a bowl, add the chicken and turn to coat well. Cover and chill for 12 hours.

2. When ready to serve, mix all the salsa ingredients together.

3. Heat the grill until hot and remove the chicken from its seasoning. Thread 4 pieces of chicken and 3 pieces of red pepper on to each metal skewer. Grill for 15 minutes, turning them occasionally, until charred.

4. To serve, warm the flatbreads in a dry pan. Place some shredded lettuce on each flatbread and then divide the chicken equally. Top with the salsa and a dollop of sour cream. Scatter over the coconut shavings. Wrap and then scoff!

Crispy John Dory with Patatas Bravas

SERVES: **4-6**

Olive oil and butter, for shallow-frying
6 John Dory fillets
75g plain flour, seasoned with celery salt, white pepper and smoked paprika

For the patatas bravas
600g potatoes
3 tablespoons olive oil
2 x 400g tins of chopped tomatoes
3 red chillies, deseeded and chopped
4 garlic cloves, crushed
Good handful of chopped parsley
Salt and black pepper

For the sauce
100g mayonnaise
100g sour cream
2 roasted garlic cloves (see page 67), squeezed from their skins
1 tablespoon Worcestershire sauce

Pair the easiest oven-baked patatas bravas recipe with crispy pan-fried John Dory for a Mediterranean fish supper. Once you see past its lethal-looking spikes, John Dory is one of the best tasting fish you can cook. Its meaty flesh is sweet, delicate and totally delicious.

1. Preheat the oven to 200°C fan/220°C/Gas 7.

2. Peel the potatoes and cut into 2.5cm cubes. Chuck away any uneven bits, so you're left with just cubes; they look nicer.

3. On the hob, heat the oil in the biggest roasting tin you have until really hot. Add the potatoes and give the tin a little shake. Season well, then pop into the hot oven and roast for 10 minutes, until they are beginning to brown.

4. Add the tomatoes, chillies and garlic, and stir well. Cook for another 25–35 minutes until the potatoes are soft on the inside but with a little bit of crispness outside. Add plenty of parsley.

5. Combine all the sauce ingredients in a bowl and set aside.

6. Heat enough oil and butter in a frying pan for shallow-frying. Dredge the fish fillets in the seasoned flour, then shallow-fry for 2 minutes on each side.

7. Remove with a slotted spoon and serve on top of the patatas bravas, with the sauce to spoon over.

Lobster Thermidor Skins

SERVES: **4**

2 large baking potatoes
80g softened butter
Salt and black pepper

For the sauce
25g butter
25g plain flour
300ml whole milk
Splash of sherry (ideally dry)
75g crème fraîche
1 tablespoon Dijon mustard
75g Gruyère cheese, grated
1 chilli, finely chopped
500g cooked lobster meat

To serve
Rocket leaves and/or chopped parsley
(optional)

Lobster Thermidor is an iconic French dish in which a creamy mixture of lobster meat is served inside the shell with a cheesy crust. Switching the lobster shells for potato skins helps to stretch out the lobster and still makes for a fantastic, luxurious baked potato. And rather than buying a whole lobster, you can pick up lobster tails instead. This dish is extremely rich, hence only serving half a spud per person.

1. Preheat the oven to 180°C fan/200°C/Gas 6. Wrap each potato in foil and bake for 1 hour until soft. Cut the potatoes in half lengthways and scoop the middles out into a bowl. Add the butter and mix well, then spoon back into the skins.

2. Melt the butter for the sauce in a pan, stir in the flour and cook for 1 minute.

3. Stir in the milk very gradually (to avoid a lumpy sauce), then bring slowly to the boil. Turn down and simmer for 10 minutes before adding the sherry, crème fraîche and mustard. Add half the grated cheese and the chilli, season well, then add the lobster.

4. Divide the lobster mixture between the potato halves. Top with the remaining grated cheese and place under a hot grill, until bubbling. Serve with a few rocket leaves and/or chopped parsley if you like.

We've been fortunate to sample a lot of different drinks over the time the show has been on air. But we both enjoy a classic cocktail. These are some of the best. Cheers!

Ian Burrell's Daiquiri

SERVES: **1**

50ml light Jamaican rum
25ml freshly squeezed lime juice
15ml agave nectar
3 dashes of Angostura orange bitters
Twist of orange peel, to garnish

1. Chill a martini glass.

2. Pour all the ingredients into a cocktail shaker and shake vigorously.

3. Strain the contents of the shaker into the chilled martini glass.

4. Garnish with a twist of orange peel, expressed so the oils of the zest gives the drink a lovely freshness. To do this hold the peel over the glass and twist it over the drink. Rub the peel over the rim of the glass before dropping the peel into the drink.

Neil Ridley & Joel Harrison's Dark 'n' Stormzy

SERVES: **1**

20ml ginger wine (such as Stone's)
Lemonade, to top up (such as Fentimans, Franklin & Sons or Fever Tree Sicilian)
50ml dark rum (such as Gosling's Black Seal)
A mint sprig, to garnish
Thin lime slice, to garnish

1. Fill a tall glass with ice cubes. Add the ginger wine and then fill the glass three-quarters full with lemonade.

2. Float the dark rum into the glass down the back of a spoon.

3. Garnish with a sprig of fresh mint and a thin slice of lime.

Karina Elias's
Monet Moment

SERVES: **1**

45ml cognac (such as Remy Martin
   VSOP Cognac)
35ml Byrrh
Dash of absinthe
Dash of sugar syrup
2 drops of Peychaud bitters
A strip of lemon peel, to garnish (optional)

1. Chill a small wine glass or goblet.

2. Throw a handful of ice into a cocktail shaker. Pour all the ingredients into the cocktail shaker and shake hard.

3. Place an oversized ice cube in the chilled glass. Strain the contents of the shaker into the glass over the ice cube.

4. Garnish with a strip of lemon peel, if using.

Carl Brown's
Cranberry Toddy

SERVES: **1**

25ml Ceylon arrack
1 cinnamon stick
1 clove
1 orange
10ml cranberry sauce
10ml runny honey
15ml freshly squeezed lemon juice
65ml water

1. Pour the arrack into a jar and add the cinnamon stick, clove and orange. Leave to infuse overnight.

2. When ready to make the cocktail, strain the arrack and remove and discard the cinnamon, clove and orange.

3. Place the cranberry sauce, honey, lemon juice and water in a pan. Place the pan over a medium heat and warm the contents of the pan, but don't let it boil.

4. Remove the pan from the heat, add the arrack and stir to mix.

5. Serve the toddy in a heatproof glass.

sweet stuff

We cook one dessert recipe on every show and a lot of the time they are the most cooked recipes by you, our lovely viewers. Often the pud is the last recipe we cook on the show, so it comes after the drinkipoos section, which brings it own challenges…

If we're being honest, on a few occasions we've cooked dessert whilst a little hazy. One time, when Lily Allen was our guest and after a particularly good drinkipoos item, we both forgot to speak while cooking the pud and there was dead air for a good few minutes.

Anyway, you can't beat a good pud and it's the perfect way to round off a meal. Collected here is a variety of simple tray bakes, fridge-friendly no-cook desserts and more fancy-pants patisserie.

Apple Crumble
Tray Bake

MAKES: **18 SQUARES**

125g butter, diced, plus extra for greasing
125g caster sugar
125g ground almonds
25g plain flour
A pinch of ground cinnamon
A splash of vanilla extract
1 teaspoon baking powder
2 eggs
3 Bramley apples, peeled, cored and diced

For the base
100g caster sugar
140g plain flour
150g ground almonds
125g unsalted butter, diced

For the top
75g flaked almonds, toasted
50g demerara sugar

To serve
Clotted cream

Combining a classic apple crumble recipe with a nutty, moist almond sponge, this tray bake is simple to make but so delicious. On the effort-to-reward scale, this charts really high.

1. Grease a 20 x 30cm baking tray and line with baking parchment. Preheat the oven to 140°C fan/160°C/Gas 3.

2. For the base, put the sugar, flour and ground almonds in a bowl, add the butter and rub into the dry ingredients until the mixture resembles breadcrumbs.

3. Tip the mixture into the prepared tray, press it down evenly and bake for 15 minutes. Remove and set aside to cool (but keep the oven on).

4. Put the butter, sugar and ground almonds in a food processor and pulse to form a crumble. Remove a couple of spoonfuls and set aside.

5. Add the flour, cinnamon, vanilla, baking powder and eggs to the processor and pulse to form a batter. Pour the batter over the cooked base and sprinkle the diced apples on top.

6. Mix the toasted flaked almonds, demerara sugar and reserved crumble mixture together, and sprinkle evenly over the apples.

7. Bake for 25 minutes, then leave to cool a little before slicing and serving with clotted cream.

Butternut Squash
& Date Loaf

MAKES: **10-12 SLICES**

400g butternut squash, cut into 1.5cm cubes
150g caster sugar
2 eggs
150ml vegetable oil, plus extra for greasing
175g chopped dates
275g plain flour
2 teaspoons baking powder
1 teaspoon ground cinnamon
150g pecans, chopped, plus extra to decorate

For the icing
150g full-fat cream cheese
50ml double cream
30g caster sugar
1 vanilla pod, seeds scraped out

When squash come into season towards the end of the year, it's time to get baking and then cosy up with a slice of this loaf cake. You can also use roasted pumpkin instead of squash.

1. Preheat the oven to 160°C fan/180°C/Gas 4. Spread the squash out on a baking tray and roast for 25–30 minutes, until soft. Remove and set aside.

2. Grease a 450g loaf tin and line the tin with baking parchment.

3. Whisk the sugar, eggs and vegetable oil together in a bowl.

4. Mash the dates and roasted squash together, then fold into the oil mixture.

5. Sift in the flour, baking powder and cinnamon, mix well and stir in the pecans.

6. Spoon the mixture into the prepared loaf tin and bake for 1 hour, or until a skewer inserted into the middle comes out clean. Remove from the oven and leave to cool.

7. Meanwhile, to make the icing, use an electric whisk to whisk the ingredients together.

8. Spread the icing onto the cooled cake, then decorate with extra chopped pecans.

Pistachio &
Lime Baklava

The classic Middle Eastern tea-time treat of layers of flaky filo pastry interlaced with chopped pistachio nuts and finished off with sugar syrup. In this version, we've added a little zesty citrus kick of lime to cut through the sweetness, but let's not kid ourselves, this is nothing but pure indulgence.

MAKES: **16 PIECES**

225g butter, melted, plus extra for greasing
300g shelled pistachios
Grated zest of 3 limes
75g caster sugar
2 tablespoons poppy seeds
Pinch of ground cloves
400g filo pastry

For the syrup
175g honey
125g caster sugar
Juice of 3 limes
Splash of orange blossom water
250ml water

1. Butter a 20cm square baking dish and line with baking parchment. Preheat the oven to 130°C fan/150°C/Gas 2.

2. Put the pistachios, lime zest, sugar, poppy seeds and ground cloves into a processor and pulse to form rough crumbs.

3. Cut the filo sheets to the size of the lined dish. Place one in the base of the dish, then brush melted butter over it and add a second sheet. Continue in this way until you have 6 layers of buttered filo.

4. Add one third of the nut mixture, then add another 6 filo sheets, brushing melted butter over each and pressing down each layer as you finish it. Continue with the layers, finishing with pastry. Lightly score a diamond or square pattern into the top of the filo.

5. Bake for 1 hour until lightly golden on top, then remove and set aside to cool.

6. Make the syrup by putting all the ingredients into a saucepan and boiling for 3–5 minutes. Pour the hot syrup over the cooled baklava, leave to cool in the tin, then cut into squares or diamond-shaped pieces to serve.

Lemon Curd & Almond Bread & Butter Pudding

SERVES: **8-10**

150g softened butter, plus extra for greasing
2 brioche loaves, thickly sliced, crusts removed
100g flaked almonds, toasted
250g lemon curd
Demerara sugar, to sprinkle

For the custard
600ml whole milk
400ml double cream
1 egg, plus 9 yolks
125g caster sugar
Splash of vanilla extract

To serve
Ice cream

We both grew up eating the classic bread and butter pudding, which was a brilliant way to use up bits of stale bread. Things have moved on since then and using sliced brioche gives this pudding a moreish richness that is beautifully offset by tangy lemon curd. Served with a scoop of vanilla ice cream, this is the traditional British pud reinvented.

1. Heat the milk and cream for the custard together, until it reaches scalding point, then remove from the heat.

2. In a heatproof bowl, use a balloon whisk to beat the whole egg and yolks with the sugar and vanilla, until combined.

3. Pour over the hot milk and cream mixture, and beat well with the whisk.

4. Butter the brioche slices and put a layer of them in a buttered baking dish, about 30 x 40cm. Sprinkle with half the flaked almonds. Dot with half the lemon curd and sprinkle with demerara.

5. Add another layer of brioche slices, followed by the remaining almonds and lemon curd, and a sprinkling of demerara. Add a final layer of brioche, followed by a sprinkling of demerara.

6. Pour over the custard mixture and leave to stand for 20 minutes. Meanwhile, preheat the oven to 160°C fan/180°C/Gas 4.

7. Bake for about 40 minutes, until golden and set, and serve with ice cream.

Pecan Slab Pie

SERVES: **6-8**

For the pastry
225g unsalted butter, diced, plus extra for greasing
350g plain flour, plus extra for dusting
1 teaspoon caster sugar
1 teaspoon vanilla extract
40–50ml iced water

For the filling
150g softened unsalted butter
225g soft dark brown sugar
3 medium eggs
150g golden syrup
150g pecans, plus an extra 100g to decorate

To serve
Cream or ice cream

Pecan pie is an American diner classic. Rather than trim the pastry case so it's neat and prissy, fold the rough edges over onto the filling before baking and serving in hefty slabs.

1. Grease a 20 x 30cm baking tin and line with baking parchment.

2. For the pastry, rub the flour, butter, sugar and vanilla together in a bowl until the mixture resembles breadcrumbs.

3. Gradually add enough iced water for the mixture to come together, then push the mixture together to form a dough. Wrap in clingfilm and chill for 1 hour. Preheat the oven 160°C fan/180°C/Gas 4.

4. Roll out the chilled pastry on a floured surface to about 25 x 35cm and about 5mm thick. Press the pastry into the prepared tin, leaving the excess overhanging the edges.

5. For the filling, use electric beaters to beat the butter and sugar together for 5 minutes. Beat the eggs in one at a time, then fold in the syrup and pecans.

6. Spoon the filling into the pastry case and fold the edges of pastry overhanging back in to form a rough tart case. Arrange the rest of the pecans on top of the exposed filling.

7. Bake for about 45 minutes, until the pastry is golden and the filling is risen and doesn't wobble – it will continue to set as it cools. Allow to cool completely in the tin.

8. When completely cold, remove from the tin, cut into squares or slices and serve with cream or ice cream.

Vanilla Cheesecake with White Peaches in Honey

A classic New York-style baked cheesecake, this is rich, dense, smooth and creamy. Admittedly, a baked cheesecake is a little more work than a stir-it-all-together-and-bung-it-in-the-fridge cheesecake, but trust us, it's worth it.

1. Line the base of a 23cm round cake tin with baking parchment.

2. Mix the fine biscuit crumb and melted butter together, then press the mixture into the lined tin and chill in the fridge for 20 minutes to firm up. Preheat the oven to 140°C fan/160°C/Gas 3.

3. In a stand mixer, or using electric beaters, beat the cream cheese and sugar together until smooth. Add the eggs and yolks one at a time, beating between each addition. Finally, add the vanilla extract and lemon juice. Mix well then pour over the chilled base.

4. Line the outside of the cake tin with foil, then place in a deep baking tray and pour water to halfway up the sides of the tin. Bake for 35–40 minutes, until just firm to the touch.

5. Mix the sour cream, milk and vanilla seeds together, pour and spread it over the top of the cheesecake and pop back in the oven for 5 minutes. Remove and leave in the baking tray until completely cool, then take out of the tray and pop the cheesecake in the fridge.

6. In a bowl, mix the peach slices with the honey to coat, and leave to sit for 30 minutes. When ready, serve slices of cheesecake with the peaches.

SERVES: **6 - 8**

300g digestive biscuits, blitzed until fine crumbs
150g butter, melted
600g full-fat cream cheese
125g caster sugar
3 eggs, plus 3 yolks
1 tablespoon vanilla extract
1½ tablespoons lemon juice
200ml sour cream
50ml whole milk
1 vanilla pod, seeds scraped out

For the peaches
4 white peaches, sliced
1 tablespoon runny honey

Lemon & Blackberry Posset with Lemon & Ginger Biscuits

SERVES: **6-8**

For the posset
750ml double cream
Pared zest (in strips) of 1 lemon and juice of 4 lemons
225g caster sugar
200g blackberries

For the biscuits (makes about 16)
125g butter
50g caster sugar, plus an extra 1-2 tablespoons for rolling out the dough
Grated zest of 1 lemon
100g plain flour
30g cornflour
50g polenta
1 teaspoon ground ginger

These little lemon pots are sweet and sharp. They are deceptively rich, so you do only need a shot glass full of posset. Serve with the biscuits. Or not. Or just eat the biscuits on their own.

1. Put the cream and lemon zest strips in a pan and bring gently to a simmer, NOT a boil.

2. Remove the zest strips, add the sugar and bring to the boil, stirring to fully dissolve the sugar. Cook for 2 minutes, then take off the heat and stir in the lemon juice.

3. Put 3 or 4 blackberries into each of 6–8 glasses, pour over the posset and transfer to the fridge to chill and set.

4. For the biscuits, cream the butter, sugar and grated lemon zest together in a bowl.

5. Add the flour, cornflour, polenta and ginger, and mix gently to combine. Roll the dough into a log, about 40–50mm in diameter, wrap in clingfilm and chill for 1 hour.

6. Preheat the oven to 140°C fan/160°C/Gas 3.

7. Cut the chilled dough into rounds, about 1.5cm thick, and dip each in the extra sugar, to coat both sides.

8. Transfer to a lined baking sheet and bake for about 12 minutes, until just turning golden. Remove and leave to set on the baking sheet for a few minutes, before transferring to a wire rack to cool completely.

9. Serve the possets with the biscuits.

Images overleaf →

Chocolate, Coconut & Date Squares

These brilliant no-bake, choccy-covered coconut and date squares are rich and decadent, with the natural sugars in the dates providing a perfect amount of sweetness. And they just happen to be vegan friendly too.

1. Line a 30 x 20cm baking tin with baking parchment.

2. Put the dates, cocoa powder, maple syrup, coconut oil and desiccated coconut in a food processor and blend until smooth. Press the mixture into the lined tin and chill in the fridge for 2 hours.

3. Place the chocolate in a heatproof bowl and bring the coconut cream and maple syrup to the boil. Pour the hot cream over the chocolate and whisk until very smooth.

4. Spoon the mixture over the chilled base and return to the fridge for another 2 hours, or until set.

5. Sprinkle sea salt and toasted coconut flakes over, cut into squares and serve with berries.

MAKES: **4 SQUARES**

For the base
600g pitted dates, chopped
110g unsweetened cocoa powder
1 tablespoon maple syrup
250g coconut oil
50g desiccated coconut

For the topping
200g vegan dark chocolate, broken into pieces
400ml coconut cream
Generous 1 teaspoon maple syrup
1 tablespoon sea salt flakes
30g coconut flakes, toasted

To serve
Mixed summer berries

Donuts with Strawberry Dipping Sauce

MAKES: **12**

50g vegan margarine
120ml soy milk
2 tablespoons sunflower oil
250g plain flour
1 teaspoon baking powder
Pinch of salt
100g caster sugar
10g ground cinnamon
Vegetable oil, for deep-frying

For the dipping sauce
250g strawberries, chopped
100g caster sugar
1 tablespoon rose water

We made these donuts for celebrity vegan Romesh Ranganathan, the comedian. Romesh said he absolutely loved them… although he had just drained every drop of all the drinkipoos cocktails immediately beforehand.

1. For the dipping sauce, put the ingredients in a pan and heat until the strawberries turn soft. Transfer to a blender and process until smooth, then strain through a sieve.

2. In a pan, melt the margarine gently over a low heat, then add the soy milk and oil and mix well.

3. Sift the flour and baking powder into a bowl and stir in the salt and half the sugar. Combine the remaining sugar with the cinnamon and set aside in a shallow bowl.

4. Add the wet ingredients to the dry and stir to combine, but don't overwork the mixture. Divide the dough into 12 and roll into balls, then press a hole through the middle of each.

5. Pour enough oil for deep-frying into a deep-fryer or wide, deep pan, making sure it is no more than one-third full. Heat to 180°C, or until a cube of white bread browns in just under 1 minute.

6. Deep-fry the donuts, in batches, for 3–5 minutes, turning once, until they turn golden and puff up to the surface. Remove with a slotted spoon and roll in the sugar and cinnamon to coat.

7. Dip the donuts in the yummy sauce to serve.

White Chocolate, Peanut Butter & Banana Blondies

MAKES: **12**

For the blondies
100g butter, plus extra for greasing
200g white chocolate, broken into pieces
1 egg
225g caster sugar
1 vanilla pod, seeds scraped out
225g plain flour
¼ teaspoon baking powder
75g peanut butter
2 bananas, roughly chopped

To decorate
100g icing sugar, sifted
1–2 tablespoons water

TOP TIP

Back in 2013, when singer Olly Murs appeared on the show, a historic moment happened that has since been commemorated by a blue plaque. While cooking a pud with us, Olly developed his now widely adopted method for folding flour into a cake batter. While working the wrist action as you fold the flour into the beaten eggs, The Olly Murs Technique™ adds a dip from the knees. This bobbing action stops you from overworking the cake mixture to ensure a fluffy sponge every time.

Take care not to overcook these blondies, as they can turn into bricks in the blink of an eye; you want to keep them a little squidgy in there. Flick the icing freestyle over the top of the blondies, like an expressionist artist throwing paint onto a canvas.

1. Preheat the oven to 150°C fan/170°C/Gas 3. Grease a 23cm square baking tin or brownie tin and line with baking parchment.

2. Put the butter and white chocolate in a heatproof bowl and set the bowl over a pan of barely simmering water, making sure the base of the bowl isn't touching the water. Allow to melt.

3. In another bowl, beat the egg, sugar and vanilla seeds together, then fold in the melted chocolate mixture.

4. Sift in the flour and baking powder, fold in the peanut butter and chopped banana, and spoon into the prepared tin.

5. Bake for 35–40 minutes, until it starts to cook on top, but is still slightly underdone – it will carry on cooking in the tin out of the oven.

6. Leave to cool in the tin, then cut into 12 pieces.

7. For the icing, mix enough of the water into the icing sugar to make a drizzling consistency, then drizzle the icing over the brownies freestyle.

Limoncello Raisin & Ricotta Cake

SERVES: **6-8**

150g golden raisins
3 tablespoons limoncello
100g butter, melted, plus extra for greasing
200g self-raising flour
200g polenta
1 teaspoon baking powder
250g ricotta
225g caster sugar
3 medium eggs
Grated zest and juice of 1 lemon
200ml warm water

To serve
Greek yoghurt
Selection of soft fruits

A little booze in a pud is no bad thing, in our eyes. Soaking the raisins in limoncello overnight means they absorb all the lemony goodness from the liqueur. The lightness and freshness of the ricotta stops the sponge becoming too dense or too sweet.

1. Soak the raisins in the limoncello overnight.

2. Preheat the oven to 140°C fan/160°C/Gas 3. Grease a 23cm springform cake tin and line with baking parchment.

3. Sift together the flour, polenta and baking powder.

4. Add the limoncello-soaked raisins, along with the ricotta, melted butter, sugar, eggs, lemon zest and juice, and warm water. Whisk together well, using an electric whisk.

5. Spoon the cake mixture into the prepared tin and bake for 55–60 minutes, until risen and golden and a skewer inserted into the middle comes out clean.

6. Allow the cake to cool in the tin before turning out onto a wire rack. Serve in slices, with Greek yoghurt and soft fruits.

Salted Popcorn Brownies with Toffee Sauce

SERVES: **6**

250g butter, plus extra for greasing
300g dark chocolate (70% cocoa solids)
4 eggs
200g caster sugar
150g light brown sugar
A pinch of fine salt
1 vanilla pod, seeds scraped out
120g plain flour
½ teaspoon baking powder
25g unsweetened cocoa powder
5g sea salt flakes
40g sweet and salty popcorn, plus extra to serve

For the toffee sauce
150ml double cream
150g soft light brown sugar
150g butter

To serve
Salted caramel ice cream

We made these brownies with George and Larry Lamb on the Sunday it just happened to be Larry's 70th birthday. These brownies are perfect to serve as an alternative to birthday cake. They're that good.

1. Preheat the oven to 160°C fan/180°C/Gas 4. Grease a 23 x 32cm baking tray and line with baking parchment.

2. Break 200g of the chocolate into pieces and place in a heatproof bowl with the butter. Place the bowl over a pan of barely simmering water, making sure the base isn't touching the water, and leave until the chocolate has melted. Roughly chop the remaining chocolate and set aside.

3. In a clean bowl and using an electric whisk, whisk the eggs, both sugars, fine salt and vanilla seeds together for 5 minutes until pale and fluffy.

4. Sift in the flour, baking powder and cocoa. Add the salt and fold in the dry ingredients, then fold in the melted chocolate and butter mixture, half the popcorn and the chopped chocolate.

5. Spoon into the prepared tin and bake for 35 minutes, then remove and leave to cool before cutting into squares.

6. While the brownies are baking, make the toffee sauce. Melt the ingredients together in a pan over a low heat, then bring to the boil and bubble for 3–4 minutes or until the sauce has thickened and coats the back of a wooden spoon.

7. Serve the brownies with the toffee sauce, extra popcorn and salted caramel ice cream.

Rose Water
Custard Tart

SERVES: 6

3 egg yolks
125g caster sugar
30g cornflour
175ml whole milk
225ml double cream
1 teaspoon rose water
1 vanilla pod, seeds scraped out
1 x 320g packet of ready-rolled puff pastry
A mixture of flour and icing sugar, for dusting

For the figs
6 figs, cut almost into quarters (leave the stem intact)
100g demerara sugar
1 teaspoon rose water

Rose water is Simon's not-so-secret ingredient that he loves to sneak into puds whenever possible. It adds a delicate, floral note and is most commonly used in Middle Eastern cooking. But you only need to add a tiny splash as you want it to be almost imperceptible. It's become such a frequent habit that Tim believes Simon has shares in a rose water producer.

1. Whisk the egg yolks, sugar and cornflour together in a pan, then slowly whisk in the milk, cream, rose water and vanilla.

2. Place over a medium heat and stir until it comes to the boil, then take it off the heat, cover the surface with clingfilm to stop a skin forming, and allow to cool.

3. Preheat the oven to 160°C fan/180°C/Gas 4.

4. Cut the pastry in half, then roll into a log, from the shorter end and cut into 12.

5. Roll out each piece into 10cm circles on a floured surface.

6. Now press a circle into each hole of a greased muffin tin.

7. Spoon in the cooled custard.

8. Cook for 20 minutes, until golden.

9. For the figs, sprinkle the sugar and rose water onto the cut side of the figs and place under a hot grill for 4–5 minutes until the sugar caramelises.

10. Serve slices of the tart with ripe figs, alongside a cup of strong coffee.

Strawberry, Watermelon & Rose Jelly Mousse

SERVES: **6**

For the jelly
3 sheets of leaf gelatine
350g strawberries
1 tablespoon rose water
Juice of ½ lemon
100g caster sugar
80ml water
150g peeled, deseeded watermelon, diced

For the fool
500g strawberries, plus extra berries, halved, to serve
150g caster sugar
Grated zest and juice of 1 lemon
500ml double cream
1 vanilla pod, split lengthways
1 teaspoon rose water
25g icing sugar

The textural contrast between the set jelly and the light-as-air mousse is what makes this summery dessert.

1. Put the gelatine in a small bowl, add cold water to cover and set aside.

2. Put the strawberries, rose water, lemon juice, sugar and water in a pan, bring to the boil and simmer for 6 minutes.

3. Add the watermelon, remove from the heat then press through a sieve into a bowl. Return the fruit purée to the pan over a low heat.

4. Squeeze the water from the gelatine and add to the pan. Stir well, remove from the heat and set aside to cool.

5. Divide the jelly mixture between 6 glass tumblers. Chill in the fridge for at least 2 hours, until set.

6. Meanwhile, for the fool, put the strawberries, caster sugar and lemon zest and juice in a pan, cover and gently cook for 6 minutes, to break down the fruit. Cool.

7. Put the cream into a bowl. Scrape the vanilla seeds into the cream, then add the rose water and icing sugar. Whisk to soft peaks, then fold in the cooled strawberry mixture, spoon on top of the set jelly and garnish with halved strawberries.

Mocha Éclairs

MAKES: **12**
each 8cm long

For the choux pastry
100g unsalted butter, diced
230ml water
130g plain flour
4 medium eggs
Pinch of salt

For the topping
50g caster sugar
50ml water
60g soft dark brown sugar
40g dark chocolate (40–50% cocoa solids),
chopped
1 tablespoon double cream
30g unsalted butter
25ml strong coffee (espresso)
200g icing sugar

For the filling
300ml whipped cream
1 vanilla pod, seeds scraped out
50g icing sugar, sifted
50ml strong coffee (espresso)

TOP TIP

Sprinkle cold water onto the baking tray after you've piped the choux pastry. The water will turn into steam in the oven and this will help your éclairs to rise.

The French word éclair means 'flash of lightning'. These will certainly be gone in one…

1. Preheat the oven to 180°C fan/200°C/Gas 6.

2. For the choux pastry, put the butter and water in a pan and simmer until the butter melts. Take the pan off the heat, tip in all the flour and mix well with a wooden spoon, until the mixture comes away from the sides of the pan.

3. Take the pan off the heat, then still using the wooden spoon, beat in the eggs one at a time (it's pretty tough on the arms, this one). Beat really well and only add the next egg once each one has been fully incorporated. Add the salt, transfer the mixture to a piping bag fitted with a large plain nozzle and cool for a few minutes.

4. Pipe 12 straight strips of choux onto a lined baking sheet, each 8cm long and 1cm wide. Bake in the oven for 30 minutes – do not open the oven door in that time, or they will collapse!

5. Take out of the oven, make a hole in the side of each using a skewer, then place back in the oven for 5 minutes more (this helps steam escape and dries out the middle). Remove from the oven and cool the éclairs on a wire rack.

6. For the topping, put everything except the icing sugar in a pan and heat until it all melts together. Take off the heat and gradually sift in the icing sugar, stirring well.

7. Whisk the filling ingredients together until stiff enough to spoon or pipe.

8. Cut the cooled éclairs in half, pipe or spoon in the filling, close up and spread on the topping.

When made a little sweeter, a cocktail can be served as dessert. But a cocktail can also be made from a dessert. These drinks are inspired by some favourite puds. Cheers!

Karina Elias's Single Origin Kentucky Coffee

SERVES: **1**

50ml bourbon whiskey
150ml freshly brewed coffee
2 teaspoons demerara sugar syrup
Double cream, hand whipped, to float

1. To make the demerara sugar syrup, heat two parts Demerara sugar syrup to one part water in a small pan, stirring until the sugar has dissolved.

2. Pre-warm a stemmed glass.

3. Pour the bourbon and coffee into the glass.

4. Add the sugar syrup to the glass and stir to mix.

5. Float a thick layer of the hand-whipped double cream on the top of the cocktail.

Ian Burrell's Fancy That

SERVES: **1**

50ml pineapple-flavoured rum (such as Plantation)
50ml condensed milk
50ml fresh pineapple juice
Nutmeg, to garnish
Pineapple slice, toasted and caramelised, to garnish

1. Shake all the ingredients with ice, strain and serve in a small wine glass.

2. Garnish with a dusting of nutmeg and a toasted caramelised pineapple slice.

Neil Ridley & Joel Harrison's Le Mousquetaire

SERVES: **1**

1 teaspoon Chartreuse herbal liqueur
60ml aged armagnac (such as Delord
    15-Year-Old Bas Armagnac)
2 dashes of Peychaud's bitters
1½ teaspoons maple syrup
Thin strip of lemon peel, to garnish

1. Pour the Chartreuse into a tumbler glass, swirl it around and then drain out to create a wash. Place the glass in a freezer to chill.

2. In a mixing glass, add the Armagnac, bitters and maple syrup, along with some ice cubes. Stir down until the ice starts to melt and the drink dilutes.

3. Strain into the chilled tumbler.

4. Garnish with a thin strip of lemon peel, expressed so the oils of the zest gives the drink a lovely freshness. To do this hold the peel over the glass and twist it over the drink. Rub the peel over the rim of the glass before dropping the peel into the drink.

Carl Brown's Espresso 'Martini'

SERVES: **1**

For the honey infusion
Runny honey
Dark chocolate (minimum 80% cocoa)
Hazelnuts
Ginger
Fresh red chillies

For the cocktail
4 tablespoons espresso coffee
4 tablespoons honey infusion (see above)
4 teaspoons ginger syrup
Whole coffee beans, to garnish

1. To make the honey infusion, a few days before your brunch party, place 2 tablespoons runny honey per drink in a jar with the dark chocolate, hazelnuts, ginger and fresh red chillies. Leave to infuse until needed.

2. To make the martini, throw a handful of ice into a cocktail shaker. Pour in the espresso coffee, infused honey and ginger syrup. Shake the cocktail shaker vigorously.

3. Strain the contents of the shaker into a martini glass.

4. Garnish with three whole coffee beans on top.

Recipe Finder

Index

Sunday Brunch
Production & Crew

CREW

Dave Skinner

Oliver Riches

Nick Harris

Ashley Spires

Tim Verrinder

Andy Jones

Helen Scott

Pete Gardiner

Naomi Callan

Julian Haynes

Belinda Marsh

Nicole Fairfield

Susie Wills

Tamara Ramsey Crockett

Hayley Boyd

Ashleigh Haines

Richard Scollard

Hannah Wing

Dominic Beresford

Kari Anne Habbershaw

Mark Isbell

Owen Billcliffe

Mark Dietz

Craig Griffiths

Olivia Newman Chant

Elizabeth Lanceman

Natalie Sanchez

Ian Rolfe

Nick Milward

Toby Deveson

John MacKenzie

Duncan Reynolds

Chris Carter

Karen Hall

Nick Webb

Chris Martin

Stewart Carter

Vasco Rocha

Duncan Elsam

Emily Tait

Jon Graves

Ed Rousseau

Jamie Shurlock

Mark Bothwick

Sebastian Leathlean

Simon Pavey

Ben Arthur

Amos Christie

Redi Baduri

Lucy Wheeler

Annabelle Law

Claire Bassano

Sarah Gardiner

Yas Othman

Janet Reeve

Gil Salter

Kirsty Thomas

Acknowledgements

Big love and heartfelt thanks to everyone involved
with *Sunday Brunch* from both of us. We've got to namecheck
Mel, Paddy, Gareth, Seb, Ben, Redi, Charlie, Michael, Alice,
Dave, Nick H and Nick M. And a special massive thanks
from me, Simon, to the brilliant team of home economists
– Claire, Yaz, Sarah and Janet – who make it look like
I know exactly what I'm doing each week. We'd also like to say
a huge thank you to the entire team at Ebury, but especially
our editor Elen Jones, for turning the dream of a
Sunday Brunch cookbook into a reality.

10 9 8 7 6 5 4 3 2 1

Ebury Press, an imprint of Ebury Publishing,
20 Vauxhall Bridge Road,
London SW1V 2SA

Ebury Press is part of the Penguin Random House
group of companies whose addresses can be found
at global.penguinrandomhouse.com

Penguin
Random House
UK

Text © Endemol Shine UK Limited T/A Remarkable
Television 2019
Recipes © Simon Rimmer, except for p96 Tim's Kung Fu
Tuna © Tim Lovejoy
Photography © Dan Jones 2019

First published in the United Kingdom by Ebury Press in 2019
www.penguin.co.uk

A CIP catalogue record for this book is available from
the British Library

ISBN 9781529102918

Project editor: Lisa Pendreigh
Designer: Louise Evans
Photographer: Dan Jones
Additional food photography: Nick Millward and
John MacKenzie for Remarkable
Food Stylists: Simon Rimmer and Claire Bassano
Assistant Food Stylist: Sarah Gardiner
Props Stylist: Tonia Shuttleworth

Colour origination by Altaimage
Printed and Bound in Germany by Firmengruppe APPL,
aprinta druck, Wemding

Penguin Random House is committed to a sustainable future
for our business, our readers and our planet. This book is
made from Forest Stewardship Council® certified paper.

MIX
Paper from
responsible sources
FSC® C018179